# THE
# SCHOOL DISCIPLINE
# FIX

# THE
# SCHOOL DISCIPLINE
# FIX

## CHANGING BEHAVIOR USING THE COLLABORATIVE PROBLEM SOLVING APPROACH

J. STUART ABLON & ALISHA R. POLLASTRI

W. W. NORTON & COMPANY
*Independent Publishers Since 1923*
New York • London

For information about permission to reproduce selections from this book, write to
Permissions, W. W. Norton & Company, Inc., 500 Fifth Avenue, New York, NY 10110

For information about special discounts for bulk purchases, please contact
W. W. Norton Special Sales at specialsales@wwnorton.com or 800-233-4830

Manufacturing by LSC Harrsionburg
Book design by Vicki Fischman
Production manager: Katelyn MacKenzie

ISBN 978-0-393-71230-8 (pbk.)

W. W. Norton & Company, Inc., 500 Fifth Avenue, New York, N.Y. 10110
www.wwnorton.com

W. W. Norton & Company Ltd., 15 Carlisle Street, London W1D 3BS

1  2  3  4  5  6  7  8  9  0

# CONTENTS

## PART 3:
## SCALING AND SUSTAINING THE SHIFT IN DISCIPLINE

# ACKNOWLEDGMENTS

This work is the product of so many contributions from our team members at Think:Kids with lots of support from the Department of Psychiatry at Massachusetts General Hospital. The book has been a long time coming. We hope you are proud of the way it reflects your efforts. It's a privilege to work alongside such a talented and passionate group of collaborators.

Thanks to the team at Norton, especially Carol Collins, who believed in this book from the start.

But the largest thank you most certainly goes to all our colleagues throughout the world who have been courageously using Collaborative Problem Solving to try to transform discipline in their schools despite all the challenges. We are honored to have had the chance to collaborate with so many dedicated, caring, and talented educators who inspire our work. Teachers are the ultimate relationship builders, skill trainers, and problem solvers. Thank you for all you do for our students with social, emotional, and behavioral challenges.

# INTRODUCTION

> *We stand together at one end of the school cafeteria, looking out on the teachers, counselors, and administrators sitting in the chairs that in a few days will be full of this year's students. We have done many trainings like this before; the image is a familiar one. Some participants look back at us, eyes bright, ready to hear about our fix for school discipline and consider applying it with the incoming class. Others look more cautious, likely wondering whether this training will result in nothing more than another binder gathering dust on the shelves in the back of the classroom. A few sit in the back looking skeptical that we will say something they don't already know.*
>
> *We look at each other, smile, and get ready to begin. It is never easy helping schools attempt to transform their disciplinary practices, but we're confident that with training, coaching, leadership, and perseverance this school, like others before, will be well on its way to a more compassionate, equitable, and effective approach that will help challenging students build the skills they need to succeed.*

Over the last several decades, we have helped countless children and adolescents who exhibit challenging behavior using the Collaborative Problem Solving (CPS) approach. This evidence-based approach was originated by Dr. Ross Greene (1998) in his book *The Explosive Child,* written for parents of children with social, emotional, and behavioral challenges.[1] CPS was initially developed for parents who wanted to reduce conflict at home because their children were displaying challenging behavior. In an early clinical trial conducted at our institution, Massachusetts General Hospital, with families who came into outpatient clinics, CPS proved to be very effective for this purpose. However, often our clinicians were hearing that some of the most challenging behaviors were occurring in school. How could we help a child struggling at school from our offices?

We began working in schools by providing consultation to teachers and administrators, to help them better understand the children we saw in our offices, and to figure out more effective ways of meeting the students' needs. In doing so, we recognized the incredible opportunity that school affords. We realized that students with challenging behavior were spending hours a day with caring, empathic, trained professionals, and CPS could be delivered at a much more consistent dose when educators were using the approach directly with these students, rather than waiting for their weekly hour in our offices. Fortunately, the same approach that worked well with parents and caregivers also provided a blueprint for educators to understand and help students with similar challenges.

Around that same time, some pioneering leaders were beginning to test CPS in their therapeutic systems and organizations, and the data from those early attempts at systemic implementation were promising as well. Since then, CPS has been implemented around the world in hundreds of therapeutic settings with remarkable results that have shifted the entire culture and approach to addressing challenting behavior in many of these programs. Entire organizations, communities, states, and provinces have embraced the approach. More recently, like therapeutic systems, entire schools have been implementing CPS to transform school discipline and effect behavior change in challenging students, and have seen great success.

In the past decade, we have taught CPS in schools of all shapes and sizes, from district schools in New York City and the largest charter school network in the United States to smaller charter networks in cities like Memphis, Tennessee and special education and therapeutic schools all over North America. All told, we train more than 12,000 educators a year in CPS. The evidence has confirmed that CPS can be used to transform traditional school discipline to a much more differentiated, compassionate, and effective approach for some of our most challenging students. The approach has helped achieve significant reductions in challenging behaviors as well as in the punitive responses like office referrals, detentions, and suspensions that do nothing to help, and may actually harm, students. The secondary benefits have included reductions in teachers' stress and improved problem-solving skills in students.

The educators with whom we have been fortunate to work have long urged us to develop some sort of curriculum; a guide to help them apply the approach and share it with others in their building. They reminded us that they are experts at implementing curricula in individualized ways with their students, and assured that with a guide like this, they would be able to spread the message of CPS wider and faster. It is our hope that the three parts of this book together provide just such a practical resource.

Part One begins with an examination of why traditional school discipline fails the students to whom it's most applied. We explain why the conventional understanding of challenging behavior is inaccurate and leads to ineffective solutions. We then use the research in the neurosciences to help explain what is actually getting in the way for students in a language we can all understand. We use this research to help educators rethink challenging behavior as a deficit of *skill, not will.* Finally, we introduce our assessment tools and teach educators how to use them in a step-by-step manner to make challenging behavior predictable and identify the specific skills deficits that cause challenging behaviors.

In Part Two, we lay out the specific steps for engaging students in Collaborative Problem Solving to effectively reduce challenging behavior while building their skills and a helping relationship with them. We begin by providing a simple framework for developing a Behavior Intervention Plan that is consistent with our *skill not will* philosophy. We then teach the steps of problem solving with students, and demonstrate how to build skills through that process. The rest of this section focuses on how to troubleshoot that problem-solving process as well as how to apply it in group settings.

Part Three is for those of you who are looking to accomplish more widespread change in your school or system, whether you are a school leader yourself or hope to engage school leaders in the mission of fixing school discipline. We begin by describing what it takes to implement CPS in an entire school, or even an entire district, by sharing our experience implementing CPS as well as what the field of Implementation Science has shown needs to be considered to effectively implement any new approach. We review the common challenges and obstacles, and provide practical solutions to them. We also describe how the approach can be used among adults; with our colleagues, with parents, and even with ourselves. Finally, we conclude with the latest research on the effectiveness of the approach.

Whether you are a teacher, counselor, coach, or administrator, reading Parts One and Two will provide you with a new mindset, a simple assessment process, and an effective intervention plan for each of your challenging students. You will walk away with strategies that are immediately actionable with the students in your life. Then, if you agree that your schoolwide approach to discipline is broken, consider gathering together to read this book in teacher teams or as a school with Part Three serving as your guide to whole-school implementation. It is only together that we can enact system-wide change that brings the latest research into action to help challenging students succeed. It is only together that we can fix school discipline.

1   Dr. Greene continues to develop his own version of the approach, now called Collaborative and Proactive Solutions, which he differentiates from our Collaborative Problem Solving approach. As of this writing, Collaborative and Proactive Solutions and Collaborative Problem Solving are identified on the Blue Menu of Evidence-Based Psychosocial Interventions for Youth (https://www.practicewise.com/Community/BlueMenu) as belonging to the same family of treatment approaches, which collectively are called Cooperative Problem Solving. Visit livesinthebalance.org for more information on Dr. Greene's work.

# THE
# SCHOOL DISCIPLINE
# FIX

## PART 1

# RETHINKING CHALLENGING BEHAVIORS

# CHAPTER 1
## WHY TRADITIONAL SCHOOL DISCIPLINE IS BROKEN

*Ms. Robbins had been looking forward to her first teaching job since she entered an education program in college. She was excited to put everything she learned in her courses into practice: instructional design, assessment, collaborating with families, ethical issues in the classroom. Unfortunately, these first few weeks hadn't gone as well as she had hoped. Although she had discussed her classroom expectations with all the students on the first day, and most of the students were doing okay, there were a few students who were ruining the learning environment for everyone. They didn't seem to care about meeting her expectations; in fact, one in particular seemed to enjoy being the student who disrupted the class every time Ms. Robbins was on a roll. Today, when she asked him to return to his seat during classwork, he said, just loud enough for her to hear, "What are you going to do about it?" Sitting at her desk after dismissal, she put her head in her hands. What was she going to do about it?*

Behavioral challenges in the classroom are a leading cause of teacher stress, departures from teaching the academic curriculum in the classroom, and talented teachers leaving the profession (Abel & Sewell, 1999; Boyle et al., 1995). Additionally, challenging behavior is also a leading predictor of a student's eventual school failure and dropout (Alexander, Entwisle, & Horsey, 1997). Everyone loses—teachers, students with behavioral challenges, and their peers—when behavioral challenges disrupt the learning environment. However, school discipline is broken.

Traditional school disciplinary practices, including rewarding positive behaviors (with star charts, merits, and praise) to increase their prevalence, and punishing negative behaviors (with demerits, detentions, and loss        ally don't work for the small        st applied! Despite all we've        develop, and what causes th        discipline remains largely u        o, relying heavily on motiv        s the incentive to behave b

Stude        n misunderstood. Thanks t        related fields, we now kno        llenging behaviors and othe        eir peers possess. Students        *disability* of sorts, but not        reading, math, or writing. Rather, these students have a learning disability in three different cognitive domains: *flexibility, frustration tolerance, and problem solving* (Greene, 2005; Greene & Ablon, 2005). If this sounds like a stretch, remember that it was not that long ago in our schools that we thought students who struggled to read were lazy or dumb, and unfortunately, we treated them that way. Now we know that the student who was trying harder than anyone else to read in class was the student to whom it was not coming naturally. The same is true for students who exhibit challenging behaviors. Those students are not *refusing to behave* any more than a child with dyslexia is *refusing to read*. They just can't.

We are currently living in the interesting lag time that always exists between when new knowledge emerges and when practices change to reflect that new knowledge. We know now beyond the shadow of a doubt that traditional notions of why some students behave in a challenging way are inaccurate. Students exhibiting challenging behavior are having difficulty handling the demands that the school environment is throwing their way. Why? Because they have trouble tolerating frustration, being flexible, and solving problems. Our response, then, should not be to provide more motivation to behave well. Those students are already motivated, whether they appear to be or not. They need more *skills*. Sadly, school disciplinary practices haven't changed yet to reflect this new information.

When schools do change their disciplinary practices to reflect what we know about why students exhibit challenging behavior, and they begin to recognize that these behaviors are signs of skills deficits, then respond by building skills in their students, amazing things happen. Teacher stress decreases. Staff turnover decreases. Job satisfaction and degree of collaboration and teamwork among educators increase. Students' behavioral challenges such as disruptive and aggressive behavior are reduced. Staff and student injuries and use of archaic procedures like physical holds and restraints in schools disappear. Symptoms of psychiatric disorders decrease. Rates of detention, suspension, expulsion, and out-of-district placement are reduced with the obvious cost savings that come hand in hand with these changes. Truancy is reduced. Family involvement and attendance increase. All this can happen by virtue of coming to a much more accurate, compassionate, humane, and effective understanding of why some students behave in a challenging fashion at school.

How do you achieve results like these? Not easily! But no change really worth making comes easily. Shifting the culture of school discipline takes time, work, resources, patience, commitment, communication, and good leadership. But so does any systemic change in a school building. Consider the relatively recent shift to differentiated instruction. When the notion of teaching to the individual student's learning style first surfaced as a goal of mainstream education, there were many skeptics. Sure, it sounded great, but . . . you have too many kids in your class to provide such individualized instruction . . . you don't have enough time . . . you have to make sure your students are prepared for mandated testing. These concerns are all quite real, and yet educators today strive to provide an individualized education for each student despite these challenges. Effective school discipline is really no different—it's just *differentiated discipline* as opposed to differentiated instruction. And differentiated discipline presents the same types of challenges: real, tough challenges, but challenges worth meeting. The high cost of not providing differentiated instruction is lack of academic progress, but the cost of not providing differentiated discipline is even higher—futures lost. In order to prevent what has been referred to as the school to prison pipeline, we need to intervene aggressively, early, and with an alternative to traditional school discipline.

Every child goes to school, and most kids with behavioral challenges show signs of their difficulties early on in school, making schools the ideal environments for early intervention and even prevention. But historically, when traditional disciplinary practices haven't worked, we have often just upped the ante and applied harsher forms of the same discipline. Zero tolerance policies are a reflection of this sad irony. When a particularly upsetting, scary, or dangerous incident happens at school, it typically is not long before you hear talk of zero tolerance. And yet a large-scale study of zero tolerance policies has proven that they not only do not work—they make our schools less safe (American Psychological Association Zero Tolerance Task Force, 2008). Again, this should not come as a surprise when we remember what research has told us about why these students behave this way in the first place. We wouldn't expect detentions or suspensions to help a child with reading challenges to read better, so why do we expect those practices to help a child with chronic behavior challenges to behave better? Then, when those don't work, we heap on more "motivation," in the form of expulsions, alternative placements, and in some schools, summonses and arrests. If these worked, rates of detention and suspension would decline over time, which is not the pattern we typically see. In fact, we sometimes have more repeat detentions than we have seats in the detention room.

So, what's the answer? The answer is to treat students with behavioral challenges the way you would a student with any other type of learning disability. Any talented educator will tell us that to effectively treat a learning disorder, you must first perform a good assessment, to figure out exactly what skills the student lacks. Then, since the standard approach wasn't working for that student, you will need a different approach to teach that student those skills in increments she can handle. The very same is true when it comes to students with behavioral challenges. Assess which skills the student lacks. Then use an alternative approach to teach those skills in increments the student can handle. This requires adjusting expectations during that skill-building phase, to be more appropriate to the students' actual skill level (See Box 1.1).

The Collaborative Problem Solving (CPS) approach is designed to help you do exactly that. This book provides a framework, language, and tools for identifying and treating challenging behavior from a skill deficit perspective. We hope you will use it as a guide to help you figure out which specific cognitive (thinking) skills related to frustration tolerance, flexibility, and problem solving your students lack. And then we'll walk you through a different approach to teaching those skills in increments the student can handle. Perhaps the best thing of all is that as you teach

| BOX 1.1. COMPARISON OF ACADEMIC AND BEHAVIORAL LEARNING DISORDERS. | | |
|---|---|---|
| | **Academic Learning Disorder** | **Behavioral Learning Disorder** |
| **Observable Behavior** | Trouble reading, writing, or doing math | Trouble meeting adult expectations for age-appropriate behavior |
| **Reason for Observable Behavior** | Skill struggles in decoding, working memory, visual processing, etc. | Skill struggles in flexibility, frustration tolerance, and problem solving. |
| **Result when Rewards and Punishments are Used to Manage Behavior** | Frustration, withdrawal, poor self-esteem | Frustration, withdrawal, poor self-esteem |
| **Useful Intervention** | Assessment of particular skill struggles. Intervention to meet student at her level and build skills in manageable increments. Adjusted expectations during skill-building phase. | Assessment of particular skill struggles. Intervention to meet student at her level and build skills in manageable increments. Adjusted expectations during skill-building phase. |

these skills, you'll find some other things happen along the way. Namely, you will create the kind of helping relationship that you'll need with your students regardless of what you are trying to help them do. Because if there is one predictor of success in helping people, it's the relationship between the helper (you) and the person being helped (your student with behavioral challenges). If you treat a student as if he lacks the will to behave better, you shouldn't be surprised when he starts to act that way. But if you treat a student as if he simply struggles with the skills needed to behave better, you'll be on your way to building the kind of helping relationship necessary to reduce the behavioral challenges in your classroom while teaching the student the skills he lacks.

The chapters that follow outline the specifics of how our team at Massachusetts General Hospital has been applying the Collaborative Problem Solving (CPS) approach in school settings. You'll see that this is not meant to be a standalone practice, or one meant to be delivered by a school counselor once or twice per week for a few minutes during pull-out time. Rather, the approach is integrated into the normal activities of the school day, and is delivered by every staff member in your building, from classroom teachers, paraprofessionals, and specialists to counselors and administrators.

CPS is also an approach to discipline that fits nicely alongside and complements other evidence-based Multi-Tiered Systems of Support (MTSS) like Response to Intervention (RTI) and Positive Behavioral Interventions and Supports (PBIS). Not unlike those initiatives, this approach is much more than just a technique; it's a mentality and a process. And it's one that your whole school community ultimately can embrace. Over time, it can be the fix for a broken school discipline system in your school or district.

The time is now to treat students with behavioral challenges with the same compassion, humanity, and effectiveness as kids with other recognized learning disabilities. We hope this book helps do just that.

# CHAPTER 2
## ALL STUDENTS WANT TO DO WELL: WHAT IS GETTING IN THE WAY?

*Melissa looked out the window of the school bus and thought about her day at school. She took out the note that her teacher asked her to bring back signed by her parents, and read it again. "Today Melissa chose to be disruptive in class. She was redirected multiple times and was warned twice that continuation of this behavior would result in a detention. After the second warning, she continued to be disruptive via horseplay, laughing, and not paying attention or facing the board. She was issued a detention, which she must serve tomorrow, after school. If she doesn't successfully complete this detention with no disruption, she will receive further consequences." Tears stung Melissa's eyes, and she sank further down in her seat. Her teacher didn't understand. Tuesdays were especially hard because the double period of math seemed to last forever. Sometimes she felt that if she had to sit in that seat quietly for another second, she would explode. And now . . . she had to sit silently in detention for an hour?! Melissa squeezed her eyes tight. "I can't," she thought. "I just can't!"*

Fundamental to CPS, and the feature that sets it apart from other school disciplinary approaches, is its philosophy. This philosophy was first described by Dr. Ross Greene in his book *The Explosive Child*, and has remained the foundation of the work that has grown out of his revolutionary ideas. The philosophy of CPS provides an anchor for all staff in a school, especially when the going gets tough, and it is very simple: *Students do well if they can* (Greene, 1998; Greene & Ablon, 2005). What that means is that a student is doing the best she can with the skills she has, and if she is not doing well, the job of educators is to figure out what is standing in the way so they can help.

On the face of it, the philosophy that *students are doing the best they can with the skills they have* sounds like common sense, right? In this case, however, common sense is actually not particularly common! The most common way of thinking about students with behavioral challenges is more like: *Students succeed if they just try hard enough.* If a student is behaving in some challenging fashion, and you believe that students do well if they just want it badly enough, then your role will be to *make them try harder,* typically through offers of rewards and threats of punishment. Most traditional school discipline is oriented around increasing students' motivation to behave in a way that will garner rewards (stars on a chart, participation points, homework passes) or avoid punishments (detention or suspension, office referrals, loss of privileges). The CPS philosophy helps educators start from a completely different vantage point. We believe that all students want to do well. So if they are not doing well, it must be more complicated than they just don't want to badly enough, or they aren't trying hard enough to behave (Greene, 1998; Greene & Ablon, 2005).

This philosophy is crucial to the approach because the more challenging the student's behavior, the harder it is to stay true to the philosophy. The more disrespectful, disruptive, and potentially dangerous a student's behavior is, the more likely the educator is to (understandably) get dysregulated as well. However, keeping this philosophy front and center helps educators to stay in the most compassionate and supportive stance when approaching the student. In our work in some of the most challenging school environments in North America, we have found that holding on tight to the understanding that *students are doing as well as they can with the skills they have* helps educators to stay regulated in these challenging moments (see Box 2.1).

| BOX 2.1. COMPARISON OF PHILOSOPHIES BASED ON WILL VERSUS SKILL. | |
| --- | --- |
| **WILL:** | **SKILL:** |
| He just doesn't want to get his work done. | Something is getting in the way of him getting his work done. |
| She wants attention, so I will ignore her to show her that it won't work. | She seems to have trouble thinking of ways to get attention in more appropriate ways. |
| He knew what the consequences were, and he did it anyway. That shows he doesn't care. | If he did that despite knowing the consequences, he really must have a hard time controlling himself. |

## THE LIMITS OF TRADITIONAL SCHOOL DISCIPLINE

Let's dig a little deeper into the assumptions behind the conventional (and incorrect) wisdom that tells us that *students succeed if they just try hard enough*. This conventional wisdom usually assumes that it is the fault of the parents when a student behaves poorly in school. Parents are blamed for being too passive, permissive, and inconsistent in their parenting, and as a result, causing their children to behave in challenging ways. Consistent with conventional wisdom, most people feel that a student who is misbehaving does so purposefully because that student has learned through interactions with her parents that doing so helps her to get something she wants or to avoid responsibility. For example, a student's silly or disruptive behavior in the classroom might be interpreted as the student trying to get attention. Similarly, a student's defiance might be interpreted as an attempt to avoid, or get out of, work. Unfortunately, psychiatry and psychology have a long history of blaming parents for behaviors and symptoms that we later learned were much more complicated. For example, mental health professionals blamed autism on a pattern of maternal behavior that was quickly termed the "refrigerator mother." Of course, that myth has been dispelled, and we understand autism spectrum disorders to be complicated neurodevelopmental syndromes. We suggest that this is true for challenging behavior as well!

The assumption that children have learned to use challenging behavior as a tool to obtain or avoid things has even been written into formal assessment procedures, otherwise known as Functional Behavior Assessments, or FBAs. Many such FBAs constrain educators to indicate whether the function of a student's challenging behavior was either to get or to avoid something. Unfortunately, if one interprets challenging behavior through the lens of this conventional wisdom, it inevitably leads to a restricted range of interventions aimed at motivating the student to behave more appropriately. Such motivational procedures often take the form of sticker charts or more complicated token economy or reward systems, which often make up a typical Behavior Intervention Plan (BIP). In this way, our false understanding of the problem (behavior motivated by a desire to get or avoid something) has led to a solution (reward or punishment) that often does not work durably.

It is worth noting here that we are not categorically critical of motivational approaches like rewards and punishments. Motivational procedures like these grew out of operant theory in psychology, and operant approaches are effective for meeting specific goals. Those goals include teaching basic expectations to students, and supplying extrinsic, or external, motivation to meet those expectations. If a student has all the skills necessary to meet certain expectations but either isn't clear on the expectations or simply needs some external motivation to do so (for instance, for a simple, time-limited, and uninteresting task such as stuffing envelopes for a one-time fundraising event), such motivational procedures can be highly effective. However, if there is anything besides understanding or motivation getting in the way of a student meeting expectations (like skills!) we might not expect such motivational approaches to be effective. In addition to not helping students develop complex neurocognitive skills, operant approaches also were not intended to promote long-lasting behavior change by building helping relationships between educators and students, increasing intrinsic motivation, or helping easily dysregulated students stay calm in the midst of frustration. But these are the reasons that the most challenging students struggle in any given school. Our most challenging students have frayed relationships with adults around them, struggle with significantly lagging neurocognitive skills, have become pessimistic about their ability to change, and get dysregulated extremely quickly. So in sum, we are not overly critical of traditional school discipline when it is used for the simple purposes that are consistent with the operant theories from which it came. We do, however, believe that we often use traditional school discipline to address things that it was never intended to work for, then are surprised when it doesn't work. In fact, it can even make matters worse.

## SIDE EFFECTS OF TRADITIONAL SCHOOL DISCIPLINE

How is it that motivational strategies can make matters worse with our most challenging students? Whether it is the promise of an exciting reward, or a threat of a pending consequence, motivational strategies activate the stress response. With easily dysregulated students, this is like throwing emotional fuel on the fire, and can trigger challenging behavior as opposed to reducing it. Some of the worst moments in our schools can be traced back to the threat of a consequence sending an already dysregulated student over the edge. Imagine the student who, frustrated by something you've asked him to do, stands pacing in a classroom, muttering about how he doesn't even want to be in your class anyway. A common response from the teacher might be, "Sit down or you can go to the office," or the even less friendly version, "If you don't want to be here, you can do this work in detention later!" How many times have you seen, in a case like this, the student in fact *not* sit down, but rather shout something back, hit a wall, or barge out of the classroom? In this case, it is not the initial frustration, but rather the threat of consequence, that puts the student over the edge. And ironically, this threat of consequence was intended to convince the child to calm down.

Perhaps even more damaging is another side effect of motivational strategies. With every motivator we send a student's way, we are also sending the message that we think the student *could* behave better if he simply tried harder. As a result, over time, this student must decide between either losing faith in educators' understanding of him, or adopting the view that he is lazy, unmotivated, and simply not trying hard enough to behave well. This is a dangerous message to send a student who ironically may be trying harder than anyone else in the classroom to behave well.

Unfortunately, school data suggest that students of color are subjected to these traditional disciplinary practices at even higher rates than Caucasian students (American Psychological Association Zero Tolerance Task Force, 2008). This is in part due to implicit racial biases that lead teachers (of all races) to misinterpret the cause of their behavioral challenges as due to modeling from parents or poor intentions and effort (Okonofua & Eberhardt, 2015). As a result, the side effects of adding emotional fuel to the fire and sending messages to the student that we believe they are lazy and unmotivated compound the risks for this already misunderstood group of students.

Fortunately, thanks to much research in the field of neuropsychology, we have a chance to do right by all the students who traditionally would have been negatively impacted by the side effects of traditional discipline. We now have a very good understanding of why traditional school discipline fails our most challenging students: Those students do not lack the *will* to behave well; they lack the *skills* to behave well. Interventions meant to target their motivation to behave well are misguided. As soon as we recognize that challenging behavior indicates a lack of skill, the picture changes entirely. The assessment and intervention process is no longer focused on the challenging behavior itself and the *function* of that behavior, but rather on the specific situations that the student has a hard time handling, and the specific skills that, if built, will help the student meet those expectations.

In Chapter 3, we will outline the assessment procedures that are specific to CPS. After that, we will describe what behavior intervention planning looks like in CPS. And then we will focus on the interventions themselves.

# CHAPTER 3
# CHALLENGING BEHAVIOR IS PREDICTABLE—
# AND PREVENTABLE

*Mr. McKay, the school psychologist, looks down at the Functional Behavior Analysis form in front of him, and then back up at Shonda. Shonda is intently scraping the laminate off the edge of her desk with a pair of scissors while Mrs. Sisson goes over the schedule for the science fair projects. Students around Shonda are starting to giggle and steal glances at her as the scraping noise continues and pieces of laminate fall to the floor, just out of Mrs. Sisson's line of sight. Shonda looks up and smirks at the students around her. Mr. McKay has seen this pattern before. He was called in to observe Shonda because of her destructive and disruptive behaviors during class. He notes down on the FBA form the behavior (desk destruction), the antecedent (Mrs. Sisson's all-group instruction and lack of attention), and the resulting peer response. Suddenly, Mr. McKay realizes that during his observations this week, Shonda's destructive behavior has only happened when Mrs. Sisson is talking specifically about the independent science projects that are due next month, verbally listing the many steps the students will need to remember to complete their projects. He thinks about how Shonda's recent neuropsychological testing revealed significantly poorer working memory than others her age. "If Shonda was better at holding a long list in her head, maybe she would have an easier time staying focused in class," Mr. McKay thinks. "Perhaps Shonda isn't trying to be destructive or to get attention from her peers; maybe she's just totally lost!" Mr. McKay looks down once again. "Now where on this form does that go?"*

A Functional Behavior Analysis (FBA) is the traditional process for assessing a student who exhibits challenging behavior at school. As the name implies, the focus of an FBA is on the challenging behavior itself. It requires an educator to observe antecedents to the behavior and to decide whether the function, or purpose, of the challenging behavior is to get or to avoid something. The assumption that this behavior was volitional is not in question. For example, disruptive behavior in the classroom may be assessed and decided to be for the purpose of gaining attention or avoiding work.

In Collaborative Problem Solving (CPS), however, the central hypothesis is that the challenging behavior is not willful or goal-oriented, but rather stems from skill struggles that interfere with a student's ability to handle a particular demand or situation. Our philosophy suggests that if a student had the skills to handle a particular antecedent adaptively, she would. Thus, the focus of a CPS Assessment is not on the challenging behavior and its functions, but rather on the circumstance leading up to the behavior and the skills deficits that caused the student to have trouble in that circumstance (See Box 3.1).

By requiring educators to name the function of an undesired behavior, conventional wisdom (will, not skill) is built into the assessment process of an FBA. Poor or misguided motivation is assumed to be the main

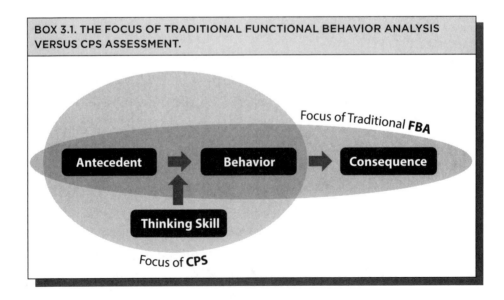

BOX 3.1. THE FOCUS OF TRADITIONAL FUNCTIONAL BEHAVIOR ANALYSIS VERSUS CPS ASSESSMENT.

driver of the behavior that is then reinforced and thus the target of the intervention. Now, an educator trained in CPS understands that motivation may still play a role. In fact, sometimes we will concede that a student may be attempting to avoid certain types of work, but we next ask the educators *why* a student would exhibit behavior aimed at avoiding certain types of work unless that work was too challenging for the student to handle in an adaptive way. In other words, we believe that if the students had the skills to complete that work successfully, she would feel motivated to do so. Thus, the target of the intervention is not increasing motivation; it is building skills. Improved motivation, and even the reduction of the challenging behaviors themselves, are direct effects of improved ability. In a CPS Assessment, the goal is to quickly shift the focus away from will, and toward skill.

Despite the differences, there are also similarities between a traditional FBA and a CPS Assessment. Educators who have been well trained in conducting FBAs are no strangers to a *situational analysis*. When conducting a situational analysis, educators ask themselves with whom a behavior occurs, at what time of day, in what specific circumstances, and over what demands or tasks. A CPS Assessment shares that focus on these antecedents to challenging behavior. In fact, understanding those antecedents will be one of the primary goals in our CPS Assessment; they are what we call the Problems, since this is what we will target with our *problem solving*.

In a CPS Assessment, the situational analysis is still the best way in which to make challenging behavior predictable. Although at first you may say, "Any little thing can set her off," or "He melts down all day, totally out of the blue," through a situational analysis, you will find that challenging behaviors are almost always predictable. The CPS assessment process is about identifying all the specific triggers, or antecedents, that typically lead to challenging behavior so that the student's behavior is more predictable. This allows you to do three things:

1. Anticipate difficulties before they happen.
2. Prioritize which problem you want to work on first.
3. Make the shift from reactive to proactive interventions.

Regardless of your intervention, you will likely agree that being proactive is preferable to being reactive. It is only with a list of predictable problems, however, that this is possible.

## THE CPS ASSESSMENT AND PLANNING TOOL (CPS-APT)

Having described the differences and similarities between a traditional FBA and a CPS Assessment, we can now proceed with the specifics of how to conduct a CPS Assessment. Included in Appendix A is a copy of the CPS Assessment and Planning Tool (CPS-APT), which is meant to take the place of the traditional FBA, to help develop a Behavior Intervention Plan (BIP) that is consistent with the CPS approach. The CPS-APT is ideally completed by a group of educators who know the student well, for example a student support team, and is best used as a discussion guide as opposed to a checklist completed in isolation. One of the main goals of the assessment process is to align all the members of the team with a common understanding of the problems and a shared game plan regarding how to approach them. If a single educator completes the CPS-APT alone, this crucial opportunity can be missed.

The CPS-APT provides basic instructions and then a place to make three lists: Problems, Skill Struggles, and Challenging Behaviors. You'll notice that the columns for these lists are arranged, from left to right, to indicate that the first two (Problems and Skill Struggles) combine to result in the third (Challenging Behaviors). However, you will actually begin completing the CPS-APT in the rightmost column, with the list of Challenging Behaviors, which is why that list is marked with #1. This list will include items such as: runs from the classroom; physical fights; disengages with head on desk; and verbal outbursts. As discussed above, this is actually the least important of the three lists, as the focus of our assessment should not, and will not, be on the challenging behavior, since that is not the target of our intervention. Remember, reduction of challenging behavior is simply a direct effect of the student being able to handle the trigger or meet the expectation. However, we still find completing this list of Challenging Behaviors critical for multiple reasons. First, a list of Challenging Behaviors is the easiest to make, and often includes the primary sources of frustration for a teacher. Allowing educators who are on the receiving end of that challenging behavior an opportunity to describe all the challenging ways that the student behaves will create an opportunity to empathize with the educators contending with that behavior. Second, this list also provides information about the severity of these behaviors that can guide other decisions, for instance, how you may choose to prioritize your interventions. Finally, because the list of Challenging Behaviors is easiest to create, it acts as an anchoring point, one to which we will return when completing the next list.

Once the list of Challenging Behaviors is completed, you will turn your attention to the list of Problems, which is marked with #2. In Collaborative Problem Solving, the term *Problems* refers to the antecedents, triggers, demands, or expectations that precipitate the challenging behaviors. Those are the situations that are typically identified in a situational analysis; *when, where, with whom*, and *over what* the challenging behaviors occur. This list is completed second because the Challenging Behaviors are the clues that will lead us to these Problems, which in turn will be the focus of our later problem solving.

The most important aspect of this list of Problems is specificity. Typically, our first try results in a list that is much too general. Our tendency is to group antecedents into overarching categories, however, the goal is actually to provide specific examples within those categories (See Box 3.2). Although we often are hesitant to be more specific because we believe the resulting list of Problems would be exceptionally long, this completed list usually tends to be less than 10 items long even with

| BOX 3.2. EXAMPLES OF PROBLEMS. | |
|---|---|
| **Not Specific Enough** | **Specific Enough** |
| Being told "no." | Being told he cannot leave the classroom during free choice time |
| Unstructured time with non-preferred peers | Sitting with peers K. G. and M. M. at lunch |
| Classwork | History or ELA classwork when requiring significant independent reading |

the most challenging students (though, of course, any of those Problems may recur multiple times during the day).

Being specific about the Problems is important for two reasons. First, it will be easier to brainstorm solutions to a specific problem as opposed to a broad or general problem. For example, it will be easier to solve a problem of "doing math homework when parents aren't home" than the problem of "doing homework." Second, this list of Problems provides the clues about which specific skills may be a struggle for that student (a topic we will cover in more detail in Chapter 4). As a detective, having specific clues is always preferable to having general clues.

When you feel your list of Problems is complete, you will return to your anchor list of Challenging Behaviors and ask, "Are there any *other* situations that lead to those challenging behaviors?" In this way, you will use your list of Challenging Behaviors to ensure that your list of Problems is complete. Remember, in making a specific and complete list of Problems, you are establishing the predictability of the student's challenging behavior. This will allow the team to become proactive in its interventions.

Use copies of the CPS-APT in Appendix A to practice making these two lists for a few of your most challenging students. Once you have completed the lists of Problems for these students, you can turn your attention to the third list: the list of Skill Struggles. This is the focus of Chapter 4.

# CHAPTER 4
# ASSESS STUDENTS' THINKING: A DEFICIT OF SKILL, NOT WILL

*Mrs. Saluja hurries the students into class. A larger number of snow days than usual this year means that statewide testing will be here before they have made it through the content for the term. As everyone takes their seats, she says above the noise: "Okay, class, take out yesterday's homework and put it on your desk where I can come by to check it off. Then open your textbooks to page 147 and write your answers to the four review questions in your notebook. When you're done, head over to the lab tables to take out today's materials." She glances around at all the students, most of whom have home-work out and are opening textbooks, pencil in hand. That is, except Serena, who looks back at her, blinking in confusion. "Oh, Serena," Mrs. Saluja mutters to herself. "Why can't that girl ever just do what she's told?!"*

In Chapter 3, we described how to complete the first two lists in the CPS-APT: the lists of Challenging Behaviors and Problems. As we discussed, the third list on the CPS-APT is what really distinguishes the CPS Assessment from a more traditional FBA. This is where your assessment becomes a functional analysis of *cognition* as opposed to a functional analysis of *behavior.* Working backwards from your list of specific situations in which the student exhibits challenging behavior (your list of Problems), the team now plays detective, guessing which specific skill struggles might explain why these situations are problematic for the student. Again, remember how philosophy guides us here. If a student could handle a situation adaptively, she would. If she isn't regularly handling a situation adaptively, it must be indicative of some underlying skill struggles.

The reason to work backwards from your list of Problems rather than just checking off skills from a list is to protect against endorsing so many skill struggles that you lose track of those that will be most helpful to address in the intervention phase. Indeed, many of your most challenging students will struggle with a host of skills found on the CPS-APT. If you simply look at our CPS Skills Reference Sheet, which you can find on the second page of the CPS-APT and duplicated in Box 4.1., you may want to check off nearly every item! However, not all skill struggles are created equal. You are definitely more interested in some skills as opposed to others. You should be trying to identify the skills that are leading to predictable problems during the course of a school day. You will be able to highlight those by using the specific situations as your clues.

As we mentioned earlier in this book, neuropsychological research over decades has helped to clarify the domains of neurocognitive skill with which challenging students struggle. When talking most generally, we say that these skills fall into the broad areas of flexibility, frustration tolerance, and problem solving. However, more specifically, there are five areas (Greene, 2005; Greene & Ablon, 2005):

- Language and communication skills
- Attention and working memory skills
- Emotion- and self-regulation skills
- Cognitive flexibility skills
- Social thinking skills

It is important to note here that the goal of our CPS Assessment is not just to identify the category of skills deficit as listed above, but rather to go further, highlighting the *specific* neurocognitive skills *within* each of these categories; this is why we have developed the CPS Skills Reference Sheet. Research in our lab has verified that assessing a child according to this list of skills can approximate the information that a much more comprehensive neuropsychological assessment can provide (Pollastri

**BOX 4.1. CPS SKILLS REFERENCE SHEET**

**Language and Communication Skills**
- Understands spoken directions
- Understands and follows conversations
- Expresses concerns, needs, or thoughts in words
- Is able to tell someone what's bothering him or her

**Attention and Working Memory Skills**
- Stays with tasks requiring sustained attention
- Does things in a logical sequence or set order
- Keeps track of time; correctly assesses how much time a task will take
- Reflects on multiple thoughts or ideas at the same time
- Maintains focus during activities
- Ignores irrelevant noises, people, or other stimuli; tunes things out when necessary
- Considers a range of solutions to a problem

**Emotion- and Self-Regulation Skills**
- Thinks rationally, even when frustrated
- Manages irritability in an age-appropriate way
- Manages anxiety in an age-appropriate way
- Manages disappointment in an age-appropriate way
- Thinks before responding; considers the likely outcomes or consequences of his/her actions
- Can adjust his/her arousal level to meet the demands of a situation (e.g., calming after recess or after getting upset, falling asleep/waking up, staying seated during class or meals, etc.)

**Cognitive Flexibility Skills**
- Handles transitions, shifts easily from one task to another
- Is able to see "shades of gray" rather than thinking only in "black-and-white"
- Thinks hypothetically, is able to envision different possibilities
- Handles deviations from rules, routines, and original plans
- Handles unpredictability, ambiguity, uncertainty, and novelty
- Can shift away from an original idea, solution, or plan
- Takes into account situational factors that may mean a change in plans (Example: "If it rains, we may need to cancel.")
- Interprets information accurately/ avoids over-generalizing or personalizing (Example: Avoids saying "Everyone's out to get me," "Nobody likes me," "You always blame me," "It's not fair," "I'm stupid," or "Things will never work out for me.")

**Social Thinking Skills**
- Pays attention to verbal and non-verbal social cues
- Accurately interprets nonverbal social cues (like facial expressions and tone of voice)
- Starts conversations with peers, enters groups of peers appropriately
- Seeks attention in appropriate ways
- Understands how his or her behavior affects other people
- Understands how he or she is coming across or being perceived by others
- Empathizes with others, appreciates others' perspectives or points of view

et al., 2018). Even just a quick rundown of this list can provide information that will be useful to guide your intervention.

Next, we will review each of these categories and give examples of specific skill struggles within them. Then we will describe exactly how to work backwards from your list of Problems to figure out which skills are the culprits of challenging behavior.

## LANGUAGE AND COMMUNICATION SKILLS

This first skills category is one that most educators find easy to understand, because it is not a stretch to see how crucial these skills are to problem solving for students. In fact, the reason the "terrible twos" fade away and don't eventually become the "terrible sixes" is primarily because neuro-typically developing 6-year-olds have developed language and communication skills that 2-year-olds do not typically possess, allowing them to express their needs without resorting to tantrums. Later in school, a student with lagging language and communication skills may have trouble letting someone know what is bothering him. He may have trouble expressing thoughts, concerns, and needs in words. However, it is important to point out that before that student can even let another know what is bothering him, he must first identify what he is thinking, feeling, or getting bothered by. He needs to talk to himself before he can express to someone else, and most of us do that in words. Finally, even before he can identify what he is thinking, he needs to accurately understand what is going on around him, and what has been said to him. All of these are individual skills that comprise the language and communication domain. Almost all of the interacting between students and adults in the school setting includes a rapid linguistic back-and-forth, requiring both expressive and receptive language skills. If a student struggles in either of those domains, these interactions as well as solving problems with other students or with adults can go awry.

It is often easy to spot when younger students are having difficulty with expressive language. In these cases, we often find adults relying on the reminder to, "Use your words!" Ironically, the students we are prompting in this way are the ones that don't have the words in the first place. By the time students get older, they have often found ways to mask language and communication skill deficits, so these skill struggles are harder to spot. For example, some students might quickly go to pat phrases such as "I don't care," or "that's dumb," and others may have learned simply to nod along as if they are taking it all in. Thus, these deficits can be challenging to identify in older students, particularly if the student performs well in the speech and language pathologist's office. Additionally, sometimes speech and language testing can miss complex language and communication skill deficits. There can be a big difference between producing as many words as you can that start with the letter S (a common task used to formally assess one aspect of language) and having to describe what is bothering you right in the moment when you are feeling bothered (a task not often formally assessed).

So how would one know if any of these language and communication skills deficits lurk below the surface? You can ask students questions to help you understand if language and communication are difficult for them. For example, when a student stares blankly at you, you might ask her what she is thinking about. If she heard and understood you and simply isn't answering because she is thinking about where she may be going for dinner, language may not be the primary issue. However, is she still thinking about what you said, trying to put together the pieces? Has she moved on to thinking about what she might say in response, but is finding it difficult to put into words? This kind of detective work can help you get to the bottom of language and communication skills deficits.

## ATTENTION AND WORKING MEMORY SKILLS

This category is hard to capture concisely, because it actually includes attention, working memory, organization, and planning, which are all related to one another. Some students with deficits in this category have a hard time focusing their attention in a sustained manner for certain tasks, particularly tasks that are not intrinsically rewarding or engaging to them. It is hard for most of us to do something in which we aren't particularly interested. Unfortunately, in school, most students have to do this quite a bit, and some struggle significantly more than others in doing so.

The ones who struggle more than others are the students with lagging attention skills.

Other students with deficits in this category have the greatest problems with working memory. *Working memory* is different from the kind of memory that helps a student remember what he did in math class yesterday. Working memory is what neuropsychologists sometimes refer to as the "cognitive shelf" in your brain. On this shelf, you can put something you need to save, and while it's there you can see it, grab it, and use it, sometimes while doing other things as well. Let's imagine that you give a student like Serena a directive that requires multiple steps like Mrs. Saluja did at the beginning of this chapter:

> *"Okay, class, take out yesterday's homework and put it on your desk where I can come by to check it off. Then open your textbooks to page 147 and write your answers to the four review questions in your notebook. When you're done, head over to the lab tables to take out today's materials."*

Serena must use her working memory to hold the request in her head while deciding how to complete the steps of the task and in what order. Ask Serena to think through potential solutions to a problem and weigh the pros and cons of each outcome? This also relies on working memory. Additionally, Serena may need to filter out noises, people, or other input that gets in the way of focusing on the task at hand, which requires good attention skills. You may be beginning to see why working memory and attention are closely related, and why, in order to efficiently organize information and plan a course of action, a student needs both good attention skills and good working memory.

## EMOTION- AND SELF-REGULATION SKILLS

The word *regulate* means to manage, or control. So, when we are speaking about *emotion-regulation skills*, we are simply talking about a student's ability to manage or control his or her emotions. In any given class, there will be students who are quite able to manage their emotional response to different situations in order to still think effectively. However, some students become overwhelmed with emotion to the exclusion of clear thinking. Specifically, some students have difficulty managing their responses to frustration, whereas other students have difficulty managing disappointment, worry/anxiety, or irritability. Some students even have difficulty controlling their positive emotional responses, such as pleasure or excitement.

In contrast to emotion-regulation skills, *self-regulation skills* refer to a student's ability to manage or control herself more globally. In CPS, we assess two common self-regulation skills deficits. The first is the ability to wait to act until thinking through the likely consequences of possible actions. You may know this ability as response inhibition or impulse control. This self-regulation skill is particularly important to understand in the context of the failures of school discipline for our most challenging students. Students with poor impulse control are the ones who tend to receive the most punitive consequences, which, again, are aimed at motivating them to behave better. However, these consequences actually require impulse control to be effective, and thus are futile as a deterrent. For example, right before Samuel is about to kick the student next to him, he has to remember that he kicked that student last Wednesday and was deprived of recess; thus, in that moment he has to decide that he doesn't want to lose recess again and control the impulse to do it again in order to avoid the same result. But if Samuel's impulse control skills are lagging, he doesn't think this all through, and instead, he kicks. Again, he loses recess. Again, his teacher hopes that losing recess will *motivate* him to think it through next time. And when calm, Samuel agrees, yes, he will try harder to do better next time. Until next time. And on and on.

The second self-regulation skill that is particularly important to understand in school settings has to do with shifting one's state of arousal, or energy, in response to a demand in the environment. All day long at school, students are asked to shift their arousal level from sitting quietly and paying attention, to working actively in a group setting, to moving about physically, to sitting still again. The elementary school student who is acting like she is still on the monkey bars five minutes into the post-recess math class is likely the student who has difficulty shifting her state of arousal. Likewise, the high school student who rests his head on an outstretched arm on the lab table while other students engage in a group project might struggle with that same lagging skill.

## COGNITIVE FLEXIBILITY

Cognitive flexibility is a category that illustrates how important it can be to focus on skills deficits rather than diagnosable conditions. While some cognitively inflexible students might meet criteria for autism spectrum disorders, for example, many students who may not meet the diagnostic criteria for any psychiatric diagnosis may still struggle with inflexible thinking to the degree that it interferes with functioning. The cognitively inflexible student tends to be a rigid, concrete, and literal thinker who thinks in all-or-none ways. These students thrive on routines and predictability. They may struggle significantly with departures from a routine, or any novel or unpredictable situation for which they do not have a template. We often describe these students as "need to know" as opposed to "go with the flow." As long as they have a template for what is to come, and as long as what comes matches that template, they do fine. Lack of a template, or a shattered template, can give rise to behavioral difficulties. As simple a change as the teacher re-assigning seats in the classroom might completely obliterate a template the inflexible child had in his mind. While other students would just move their existing template to the new desk (sit down, take out homework), for the inflexible child, that old template no longer exists. He must start over. He doesn't know what to do. In addition, these students often display a perseverative style of thinking where they get stuck on an idea, an answer, a thought, or a desire, and have a hard time moving off of it.

A specific form of all-or-none thinking that causes difficulty for students is something called cognitive distortions, or thinking traps. These are inaccurate interpretations of information that often lead to challenging responses. The father of cognitive therapy, Dr. Aaron Beck, identified several thinking traps, such as personalizing, catastrophizing, and overgeneralizing (Beck, 1976; Burns, 2012). A list of these distortions, and common examples that you may recognize in your students' thinking, can be found in Box 4.2. While there is usually a grain of truth in most cognitive distortions, they do not accurately reflect reality. For example, the student who says, "nobody likes me" is probably *not* the most popular kid in class. However, it may be that *somebody* in the class likes him! A "gray" view of the information, such as "I'm not the most popular, but at least I've got a couple friends," would be a lot more adaptive than the black-and-white interpretation of this inflexible thinker.

**BOX 4.2. COMMON EXAMPLES OF COGNITIVE DISTORTIONS HEARD FROM STUDENTS WITH DEFICITS IN COGNITIVE FLEXIBILITY.**

| Example | Type of distortion(s) |
|---|---|
| "She always gets to go first!" | Over-generalizing |
| "Kids here don't like me!" | Mind reading |
| "I'm terrible at math." | All-or-nothing thinking |
| "I can't trust anyone!" | Over-generalizing |
| "They look like real athletes in gym, and I look like a big loser." | Magnifying, Labeling |
| "I know I will fail the test." | Fortune-telling, Catastrophizing |

Some of the most challenging cognitive distortions are the ones borne of trauma. For example, students with significant trauma history may believe that, in order to protect themselves, they cannot trust anyone at school. While such a distortion may have been protective in an abusive environment, it becomes less adaptive in a trusting school environment. In these cases, simply altering that particular distortion and encouraging the student to think in a more nuanced way is unlikely to be effective, unless it occurs in the context of a trusting, helping relationship. We will talk more about responding to trauma in Chapter 8.

## SOCIAL THINKING SKILLS

Many of the skill struggles described above can lead to problems in social situations. However, there are additional skills deficits that are purely social in nature. These involve even the most basic social skills, which aren't basic to some students, such as how to start a conversation, join a group, gauge whether someone is interested, and be reciprocal in an interaction. More complex social thinking skills involve the capability to understand the impact of your own behavior, and to take another person's perspective. Many students who struggle in these areas have what we refer to as a broken feedback loop. We all rely on our feedback loops to gather information as to how we are coming across and to determine whether we need to change our behavior. Some students may not gather any data, or may gather it incompletely, or may interpret the data inaccurately. We have all met the student who doesn't seem to know when "enough is enough," whether that is rough housing during physical education class or joking during class. Knowing when enough is enough requires an intact feedback loop, the ability to read people's responses and change behavior accordingly.

It is not uncommon for educators to guess that a student with social thinking skills deficits is misbehaving in order to seek attention. The underlying philosophy of CPS reminds us that if a child could garner attention in an adaptive way, she would. So, if she is having difficulty seeking attention in a way that doesn't cause problems, it is likely that she struggles with many of the skills described above that would be required to do just that. Incidentally, we do not subscribe to the commonly held belief that negative attention is better than no attention at all. While neither sounds great, we believe most of us would prefer to be ignored than to have others constantly upset with us. These are but a few examples of the myriad social thinking difficulties with which behaviorally challenging students struggle.

## IDENTIFYING SKILLS TO BE BUILT

Now that we have reviewed examples of skill struggles in the five domains listed above, let's return to how best to identify them. Remember that you want to work backward from your list of Problems on the CPS-APT; the list that contains the specific situations in which the challenging behavior occurs. Ask yourself or your team: At what skill(s) would the student need to be better in order to handle that specific situation more adaptively? Let's consider two examples.

## Example 1: Benjamin

Benjamin's school support team has gathered to begin assessing his needs for the coming school year. In relaying the specific situations that lead to Benjamin's challenging behavior, his homeroom teacher, Mrs. Colella, describes him as "Dr. Jekyll and Mr. Hyde." She says, "You never know when he is going to blow. He can be a leader in the class one minute and incredibly disrespectful the next!" Asked for a specific situation in which he has been challenging, Mrs. Colella describes an estimation task during math class today, in which each student was asked to guess how many gumballs were in a jar. Benjamin refused to participate, calling the task stupid. "See?" Mrs. Colella says to the team, "This came out of nowhere! He said it was stupid to guess the number of gumballs because he could tell me *exactly* how many were in there, if I would just let him count them!" She goes on to tell everyone about another activity she planned, during which students would pretend to be migrant workers, sitting on the floor for snacktime instead of at their desks. Benjamin said this activity was terrible, and refused to eat snack with the class, instead sitting alone at his desk. The team reviews the CPS Skills Reference Sheet, and begins to guess where Benjamin struggles. By listening to a few different stories, they begin to see patterns, and can make educated guesses about the skills deficits behind them. Certain skill struggles stick out as the culprits leading to trouble with those specific situations.

Notice how making educated guesses about skill struggles is much easier when using specific situations as clues, as opposed to the challenging behavior that ensues. Had we simply told you that Benjamin says disrespectful things during class, you may have wondered whether he has difficulty with the language and communication skill of articulating what's bothering him. However, in this case, that would not be accurate. When asked in a calm moment later in the day, Benjamin has no difficulty articulating why he thought these activities were "stupid" and "terrible." Benjamin is calm and articulate until he is asked to do gray, ambiguous thinking. Then, because of a primary difficulty with cognitive flexibility, he becomes emotionally dysregulated and loses his ability to express his concerns. While Benjamin may benefit from building skills in all these areas, it is improvement in cognitive flexibility that will likely lead to the greatest improvement. See Box 4.3 for the three lists the team made on Benjamin's CPS-APT.

| | PROBLEMS | SKILL STRUGGLES | CHALLENGING |
|---|---|---|---|
| PLAN A, B, or C | The situations WHEN the child has difficulty. Also known as expectations, precipitants, antecedents, triggers or contexts that can lead to challenging behavior. When making your list, describe the who, what, when and where and be specific! | The reasons the child is having difficulty handling these specific situations. Use the list of problems as your clues and refer to the list of skills on the next page. If the problems are the WHEN, the skill struggles are the WHY. | BEHAVIORS The challenging behaviors are the observable responses that often bring up the greatest concerns for adults and parents. Examples are yelling, swearing, refusing, hitting, crying, shutting down, etc. |
| | - Estimation tasks in math class- e.g., guessing number of gumballs<br>- Being asked to have snack in a different place during an enrichment activity | - Seeing shades of gray<br>- Handling uncertainty, ambiguity<br>- Deviating from routines<br>- Managing frustration<br>- Expressing his thoughts and needs in words | - Calling classroom activities 'stupid' or 'terrible'<br>- Refusal to participate in classroom activities<br>- Withdrawal form peers and teacher |

**BOX 4.3. STARTING BENJAMIN'S CPS-APT.**

## Example 2: Shauna

When Shauna's student support team gathers to discuss what has been going on with her, common complaints are that she is disruptive and offensive in class, frequently derailing the teaching and focus of the other students. Shauna's chemistry teacher states that Shauna appears to be seeking attention with her negative behavior; she often arrives 10 minutes late to class, and begins disrupting other students as they are doing their do-nows, which are the short pieces of classwork meant to orient the class to the upcoming lesson at the very start of class.

Like Benjamin, Shauna may have a cluster of skills deficits that all contribute to the challenging behavior, but we want to understand which are primary. At this point in the conversation, leading possibilities of Shauna's skill struggles include the attention and working memory skills required to plan ahead and manage time effectively to arrive at the beginning of class. In addition, Shauna might struggle with shifting her arousal level from whatever she was doing between classes to quickly settling into quiet do-now work. Finally, it seems plausible that she is having a difficult time understanding the impact her behavior has on the other students, not to mention her teacher.

Shauna's teachers continue describing other specific situations in which she exhibits challenging behavior. They almost universally describe extremely poor homework completion. She often does not bring her required materials home, and if she does, they rarely make it back. Consulting the list of hypothesized skill struggles, the team decides that in combination with her behavior during do-nows, it seems Shauna may have primary deficits in attention and working memory skills, and secondary deficits in self-regulation and social thinking skills. See Box 4.4 for the preliminary list the team made on Shauna's CPS-APT.

Even once the team has more confidence in their understanding of Shauna's primary skill struggles, they acknowledge that these are still hypotheses. Soon enough, they will be doing Collaborative Problem Solving with Shauna, and will see where she gets stuck in the problem-solving process, which will also help improve their understanding of Shauna's particular skills deficits. During the initial assessment, however, there is no need to worry about getting this list of Skill Struggles exactly right. The primary purpose of this list is to promote a compassionate, skills-oriented view of Shauna. As we discussed earlier, that shift in thinking is critical to being able to implement CPS successfully with the most challenging students. Understanding why a student behaves in

| | BOX 4.4. STARTING SHAUNA'S CPS-APT. | | |
|---|---|---|---|
| **PLAN A, B, or C** | **PROBLEMS** The situations WHEN the child has difficulty. Also known as expectations, precipitants, antecedents, triggers or contexts that can lead to challenging behavior. When making out list, describe the who, what, when and where and be specific! | **SKILL STRUGGLES** The reasons the child is having difficulty handling these specific situations. Use the list of problems as your clues and refer to the list of skills on the next page. If the problems are the WHEN, the skill struggles are the WHY. | **CHALLENGING BEHAVIORS** The challenging behaviors are the observable responses that often bring up the greatest concerns for adults and parents. Examples are yelling, swearing, refusing, hitting, crying, shutting down, etc. |
| | - Transitioning from hall to class<br><br>- Bringing materials home to do homework<br><br>- Handing in homework | - Planning and organizing<br><br>- Keeping track of time<br><br>- Shifting state of arousal<br><br>- Understanding the impact her behavior has on others | - Arrives late to class<br><br>- Barges into class loudly<br><br>- Distracts others from do-nows by talking<br><br>- Failing due to missed homework |

a challenging way is regulating in itself, and also helps us avoid taking the behavior personally. Rather than viewing challenging behavior as an affront to authority, we come to see it as no different than an academic struggle that a student might have in class.

## FREQUENTLY ASKED QUESTIONS ABOUT SKILL STRUGGLES

We are often asked whether there are *ever* times that we think a student is simply misbehaving because he or she doesn't *want* to do something. Are there *ever* times when this may be the case? Of course! First of all, remember what we said earlier that not having the skills needed to do something is one way to decrease motivation for doing that thing, whatever it is! Additionally, just like you, all students have occasional times when, for whatever reason, they just may not feel like cooperating with the expectation, *whatever* it is. However, we have come to learn that it is fairly difficult to tell the difference between a lack of will and lack of skill, particularly in the heat of the moment. When a student's challenging behavior is frustrating to us, we are unlikely to be in a state of mind to come to an unbiased assessment of the cause. As a result, we suggest taking the safer route. If you treat a student as if he is lacking skill not will, and collaborate to try to solve a problem, there aren't a lot of downsides. However, the reverse is not true. If you mistakenly assume that a child just doesn't want to comply when actually he lacks the skills to do so, significant harm can be done.

Another common question concerns the inconsistency of a particular student's behavior. When discussing potential skill struggles, you will undoubtedly hear members of the team argue that there cannot be a lack of skill because they have seen the student meet that expectation using those same skills on another occasion. For example, a teacher may state that she knows Justin should be able to handle a difficult peer in algebra because they sit next to each other just fine in digital photography class. This is where it is absolutely crucial to understand, first of all, that all skills exist on a continuum. It is unlikely that a student possesses or lacks a skill entirely. Where the student is on the continuum at any particular time may shift depending on the situation or context, and the resulting state of arousal of their brain. Certain situations will help to keep a student well regulated so that he can access his skills easily. A different situation or context, however, might lead to significantly more dysregulation, and all of a sudden, the skills that student evidenced just the day before are nowhere to be found. Perhaps the girl Justin wants to ask to the prom sits in front of him in algebra. Perhaps algebra is at the end of the day, when Justin is tired, or perhaps algebra is a particularly challenging subject for him. Any number of things could alter the context so that the social and emotion-regulation skills that Justin exhibits in one class are not available to him in another.

# CHAPTER 5
## DEVELOP A GAME PLAN: THERE ARE ONLY THREE OPTIONS

*Mr. Ziegler was tired of battling with Amit when it was time to end indoor recess and get back to work. He regretted telling the fourth-grade students they could bring in activities from home when the weather was too wet to go outside. Just like some of the other students, Amit brought in trading cards. But, more than the others, getting Amit to put away his cards and refocus on schoolwork was a real challenge. Plopping down at a staff room table for a quick lunch, Mr. Ziegler mulled over his options. What he wanted to do was tell Amit that he can't bring his cards anymore—but he didn't really want to deal with the tantrum that would surely ensue, or ruin the good relationship he had been working on building with Amit. Maybe he should just ignore the problem and let Amit play right through the period after recess. Amit would stop eventually, right? Mr. Ziegler sighed. He couldn't do that in good conscience; Amit was already behind in a number of subjects, so missing more work wasn't really an option. Mr. Ziegler wondered if there was anything else to do. He was looking for a solution that would solve this problem for good, avoid a meltdown, keep a good relationship with Amit, and help Amit get better at transitions. Next year's teachers will definitely not be as forgiving, so Amit had better learn these skills now.*

Before we discuss what to do when expectations aren't met, let's first take a few moments to make sure we are setting expectations in a way that maximizes students' abilities to meet them. Remember that all children (and educators!) need clear expectations to be part of a successful school. We don't know of any setting that puts large groups of children together that does not need clear and realistic expectations. In fact, sometimes there can be a fair amount of chaos in a classroom, not because it is a class full of students with skill struggles, but because the expectations are not clear, or they are unrealistic, or they are a moving target. Students can't meet your expectations unless they are aware of what the expectations are!

The teaching of expectations involves frequent reminders of what's expected of students at any given point in the day, whether that be the expectation for circle time, in line at the cafeteria, on the bus, or in the biology lab. That is, expectations must be *clear.* If you have spent any time in a kindergarten classroom, you might notice that teachers are constantly reminding children what's expected of them. A kindergarten teacher we worked with told us that there is a very good reason for this: If she constantly reminds students to keep hands to themselves, and then a student isn't keeping his hands to himself, she can be sure that it is not because he is unaware of the expectations; there must be something else going on. Something else—like skill struggles! But we cannot confirm that the reason a student isn't meeting expectations is due to skill struggles until we know that the student is aware of the expectations.

In addition to being clear to the students, expectations have to be developmentally appropriate, and thus *realistic.* If the expectations in a mainstream classroom are realistic, the vast majority of students should meet them the vast majority of the time. If many of the students struggle to meet many of the expectations in a classroom, that is a clue that the expectations are likely unrealistic or unclear.

We find that it is always much easier to implement CPS in a school that does a good job with setting clear and realistic expectations. For example, we will talk later in this book about integrating Positive Behavioral Intervention and Supports (PBIS) with CPS. If a school has successfully implemented PBIS, that usually means that they do a good job setting clear and realistic expectations with students, which makes our job much easier. Effective PBIS helps highlight the children with skill struggles, because they are the ones not meeting the clearly stated, appropriate expectations at school.

To review, if a classroom has realistic expectations that are taught clearly to the students, most of those expectations will get met by most of the students most of the time. If the expectations in a classroom are taught clearly to the students, and they are realistic, and some students aren't meeting them, we can be confident that we have problems to solve and skills to train. Remember, *problems to solve* are the situations in which expectations are not being met. And when you have a problem to solve, you need a plan for solving it. Next we will discuss your options for handling those problems. However, before we do, we want to reflect on what goals we might be trying to pursue.

## YOUR FIVE GOALS

In our work with many schools over the last couple of decades, we've been struck by the consistency of the goals that educators have in working with challenging students. Certainly, the most practical goals involve helping students meet school and classroom expectations, reducing the amount of challenging behavior in the classroom that is disrupting learning, and solving chronic problems so everyone isn't dealing with them each and every day. Beyond those immediate goals, however, once educators come to understand challenging behavior in the terms of skill struggles, an additional goal becomes clear: helping the student build skills that are needed for solving problems on his or her own. Building skills will remediate the "learning disability" that is getting in the way of that student meeting expectations, and as a result, will help build the student's confidence and sense of competence, which are linked to internal drive for success. Finally, most educators have seen firsthand the importance of a good relationship with students and would agree that maintaining or improving the quality of that relationship is another reasonable goal, and research has demonstrated that there are particular characteristics that both therapists and teachers say are critical in order to have a good helping relationship and to facilitate change (Martin, Garske & Davis, 200; Soper & Combs, 1962). These five goals, then, are summarized in Box 5.1. These are the goals of good discipline; the goals we aim to achieve with our most challenging students.

| BOX 5.1. THE FIVE GOALS OF GOOD DISCIPLINE. |
| --- |
| **1.** Pursue your expectations |
| **2.** Reduce challenging behaviors |
| **3.** Solve chronic problems so they don't keep occurring |
| **4.** Build skills (and thus confidence and internal drive) |
| **5.** Build, or maintain, a helping relationship |

## YOUR THREE OPTIONS

Finally, it is time to discuss planning the intervention you will use when the expectations aren't being met. Pick any Problem on any student's list, and ultimately you really have only three options for how to handle it. In the first edition of *The Explosive Child*, Dr. Ross Greene referred to these options as Baskets, to represent the image of placing each problem into one of three Baskets (Greene, 1998). As Collaborative Problem Solving moved beyond a parenting approach and into other settings, those options were referred to as Plans A, B, and C (Greene, 2005; Greene & Ablon, 2005), labels that have stuck among practitioners and will be used throughout this book. Whatever you call them, the three options are these: You can try to make the student do what you want him to do (Plan A); you can try to solve the problem together with the student in a way that works for both of you (Plan B); or you can drop your expectation for now and handle it the way the student wants it handled (Plan C). Note that if only the **A**dult's concern is taken into account, you are using Plan A. If only the **C**hild's concern is taken into account, you are headed for Plan C. How do you know when you are doing Plan B? You take into account **B**oth sets of concerns (Greene, 2005; Greene & Ablon, 2005). These three Plans are summarized in Box 5.2.

| BOX 5.2. THREE OPTIONS FOR ADDRESSING AN UNMET EXPECTATION. | | |
|---|---|---|
| **Plan** | **How do you handle the problem?** | **Whose concerns are met?** |
| A | Impose your will | Adult |
| B | Solve the problem collaboratively | Both |
| C | Drop it – for now | Child |

**PLAN A.** When a student isn't meeting expectations, can you guess what the most common adult response is? If you answered Plan A, you are right. However, let's consider that on the heels of having established the importance of the five goals of good discipline in Box 5.1. Does Plan A attempt to pursue your expectations of the student? Absolutely! In fact, this is why Plan A is so popular. As we mentioned above, our expectations of students are very important. So when a student doesn't meet one of our expectations, we want to do something about it. However, let us make an important clarification: Plan A does not *guarantee* that your expectation will get met. Interestingly, many of our most important expectations are not ones that can be imposed, even if we wanted to. For instance, how would you *impose* that a student arrives on time to class? You can demand, cajole, threaten, and bribe, all of which may be part of Plan A. But when the student *still* doesn't arrive on time, short of finding her before class and physically dragging her in (we are not recommending this strategy!), you may be out of options!

Let's see how Plan A does with the other four goals: Does it reduce challenging behavior? Most educators will say sometimes it will, but also are quick to point out that even if it reduces the challenging behavior temporarily, that challenging behavior will likely be back next time you set the same expectation. Perhaps more important, however, is that not only does Plan A not necessarily reduce challenging behavior, but it often directly causes challenging behavior. As we discussed in Chapter 2, the threat of imposing your will is not particularly calming with students who are prone to rapid dysregulation. In fact, Plan A often throws emotional fuel on an already simmering fire, leading to some of the worst moments in our school buildings. Does Plan A solve chronic problems so they don't keep coming up? Not so much—if it solves the problem, the fix is usually temporary. Is there anything about imposing your will on a student that helps her build neurocognitive skills? No. And how does Plan A do at helping build or restore a helping relationship with the student? It's hard to imagine how a relationship heavily characterized by imposition of will could feel like a helping relationship to the student. So in summary, Plan A is an attempt to get your expectations met, but comes at a cost to the other four goals.

It is important to note that Plan A does not always have to be harsh. Any attempt to solve a problem in a way that addresses only the educator's concern qualifies as Plan A. For example, you could try to impose your will upon a student by calmly explaining why it is necessary. We call that Plan A plus logic! With very young students, another popular version of Plan A is when you count to three when the student is not meeting your expectation with the consequence to follow if they do not comply. That is simply Plan A with a three second warning!

**PLAN C.** In Plan C, the adult makes a thoughtful decision to drop an expectation for the time being, or to solve a problem the way the student wants it to be solved. For example, perhaps Damian has trouble completing homework, but gets dysregulated and defensive when you ask him about it. You happen to be working on some other pressing problems with Damian this week or this just isn't a good time to bring it up. You may decide to accept Damian's partially complete assignments without addressing the problem—for now. Plan C is deciding what you're working on and what you're not yet working on. It is prioritizing your Problems in advance of them coming back up, and prioritizing is a crucial component of any successful Behavior Intervention Plan. With Plan C, although you may have decided to solve the problem in the way that addresses the student's concern and not your own (for example, accepting Damian's incomplete homework while you wait until you are ready to make a better plan), that does not mean the student is in charge. The team is in charge, because it is the team deciding which expectations to drop for now. One final note about Plan C: The shortcomings of Plan

A (particularly the increase in challenging behavior that often follows) can lead educators to a pattern in which the educator tries to impose their will, the student escalates, and the adult bails. At first glance, this may look like Plan C. However, this represents a common and serious misconception. Plan C is not giving in or bailing after a failed attempt at Plan A! Plan C must be strategic.

When used strategically, which of the five goals does Plan C pursue? Plan C is very effective at reducing challenging behavior. If you drop an expectation that is frequently resulting in challenging behavior, you will get less challenging behavior. That is the benefit of Plan C, which is not to be underestimated. With a student who is particularly out of control in a classroom, the first goal should be stability, and Plan C is an effective stabilizer. The disadvantage of Plan C is that it is not a long-term solution. Plan C does not help you pursue an expectation that is important to you, because you must set that expectation aside for now. Plan C hasn't solved that problem durably. There is nothing about dropping an expectation that builds neurocognitive skills. And while dropping an expectation can have positive impact on a relationship by reducing conflict, it also does not build a helping relationship in which educator and student are digging in together to work on solving hard problems. So like Plan A, Plan C pursues only one of our five goals.

**PLAN B.** This leaves Plan B. Which of the goals does Plan B pursue? When trying to solve a problem collaboratively with a student in a way that works for both of you, you are pursuing your expectation, reducing the likelihood of triggering challenging behavior, working toward a durable solution, and, as we will explore in Chapter 7, helping the student practice a vast array of cognitive skills, all embedded in an empathic process that builds a helping relationship. See Box 5.3 for a quick reference to which Plans address which goals.

Educators sometimes tell us that they tried Plan B and it "didn't work." When we ask what they mean, they explain that the student still isn't meeting their expectation. In these instances, we like to clarify that neither Plan A nor Plan B *guarantees* getting your expectation met, though of course in both cases, you are making an attempt at it. But if you are going

**BOX 5.3. THE THREE PLANS AND THE GOALS ADDRESSED BY THEM.**

| Goal | Plan A | Plan B | Plan C |
|---|---|---|---|
| 1. Pursue your expectations | x | x | |
| 2. Reduce challenging behaviors | | x | x |
| 3. Solve chronic problems | | x | |
| 4. Build skills (and thus confidence and internal drive) | | x | |
| 5. Build or maintain a helping relationship | | x | |

to pursue your expectation without a guarantee of getting it met, why not choose the plan that keeps the student calm, practices skills, gets closer to solving the problem durably, and builds a helping relationship (Plan B), as opposed to the plan that is more likely to set off challenging behavior, definitely won't solve the problem in a durable way, doesn't practice skills, and gets in the way of building a helping relationship (Plan A)?

## A WORD ABOUT MOTIVATION

Let's think more about the goal of building internal drive in our students, which is part of our fourth goal. You may know that there has been a recent backlash against the practice of rewarding children for every good turn, and for the now-pervasive practice of giving every child a participation trophy. Motivation researchers have long found that offering rewards for a job well done (or just a job done at all) often has the ironic effect of decreasing students' internal motivation to perform that job (Deci, Koestner & Ryan, 2001). This is similar to what happens to professional athletes when they start making money to play, and they find that the passion and drive for the game that they felt in high school and college begin to melt away.

When an individual gets rewarded for an action, that individual starts focusing more on the reward than on the natural pleasure that the action may bring them. Remove the reward, and they are actually *less* likely to perform the action than they would have been if they'd never been rewarded at all. In contrast, research (Ryan & Deci, 2000) has also found that there are three factors that foster sustained internal drive in us humans: competence ("I can do this"); autonomy ("I have control over what happens here"); and relatedness ("I am connected to people around me"). Plan A is not a particularly good recipe for fostering these factors, especially when Plan A comes in the form of sticker charts, points, and other systems of rewards and consequences that attempt to manipulate a student's behavior through mechanisms of power and control—the opposite of building a sense of autonomy. Plan C doesn't do a good job of this either, because while reducing expectations has advantages such as helping avoid challenging behavior, it does not leave the student with a sense of accomplishment and thus competence. We think you will come to find that Plan B provides a great recipe to foster internal drive, by helping students learn the skills (competence) to solve problems independently (autonomy) through an empathic interpersonal process (relatedness).

## MAJOR MISCONCEPTIONS

Imagine this scenario: The bell has rung and you are ready to start class. Two students are loitering in the halls, and you don't want to start class without them for multiple reasons. You go to the door and say to them emphatically: "Class is starting. You need to come inside now!" Which Plan is that?

> Plan A (impose your will)?
> Plan B (collaborate)?
> Or Plan C (drop it for now)?

In our experience, having provided this scenario and asked this question to thousands of educators, we find that nearly everyone has the same answer: Plan A! And yet, this was actually a trick question. It was not Plan A. Or Plan B. Or Plan C for that matter. What was it then? You were simply stating your expectation! And stating an expectation is different than imposing your will when the student doesn't meet that expectation. In other words, the Plans are used when you have an *unmet expectation*, and you can't have an unmet expectation until you have an *expectation* in the first place.

Recall that at the start of this chapter we described how important it was to have clear expectations for your students. Setting those clear expectations is crucial and is not Plan A! Plan A is one of the three options you have for an intervention once you have set a clear expectation and a student is not meeting it—not when they haven't met it just once, but when they aren't meeting the expectation chronically. If a student is late to class with any regularity, and you have clearly set the expectation of on-time arrival, that should go on the list of Problems on the student's CPS-APT, allowing you to decide proactively how you will handle it (with which Plan) moving forward.

> **Stating an expectation is different than imposing your will when the student doesn't meet that expectation.**

Clearing up this fundamental misconception is critical. Every school with which we've worked has had moments of confusion around this issue, which inevitably led to some chaos and for which people were unfortunately apt to blame the approach. It frequently goes like this: Educators confuse Plan A with setting expectations. They try hard to avoid Plan A, given the downsides described earlier in this chapter. In their efforts to do less Plan A, they stop asking students to do things, or at least fear they can't, and this leads to total chaos in the classroom.

Inspiration for the scenario above came directly from a classroom we visited, in which the teacher was struggling to implement CPS. When we stopped in, the teacher was visibly frustrated by the students congregating outside the door of the classroom when the bell rang. We asked her how she planned to handle the situation. She exclaimed: "I don't want to use Plan A!" We were happy to hear that, and asked what she planned to do instead. She said she didn't know. We asked if she had gone to the door yet and asked the students to come inside. She repeated: "I told you I didn't want use Plan A!"

Right there and then, we knew the reason for the recent chaos we had heard was occurring in her class: This teacher was confusing setting expectations with using Plan A. In her efforts to do less Plan A, she felt like she couldn't ask her students to do anything at all. Poor teacher! No wonder things got so out of control in her class, and she felt so powerless and wasn't a fan of the approach. CPS does not mean anything goes! Structure in the form of clear expectations is crucial to any well-run classroom. But don't confuse the structure itself with responses to that structure when students don't adhere to it. If your expectations aren't met, then you have three options: Impose your will, collaborate on a solution, or drop the expectation for now.

You might ask: "Okay, so at what point does setting an expectation become Plan A?" The answer is that it becomes Plan A as soon as you try to impose your will to *make* the students come inside, which might look like anything from threatening a detention if they don't comply to taking them by the arm and walking them inside—we've seen both! A warning, however: While it may not officially be Plan A, if you state your expectations harshly enough, it can still cause what Plan A causes—challenging behavior. For example, you are likely to get a different response to, "Come on in now please. I don't want to start class without you," as opposed to, "You need to get in my classroom now! Do you hear me?!" Both are, technically speaking, setting an expectation, and are not Plan A, but the second is still more likely to cause challenging behavior. This is especially true

*You do not get Plan B by mixing a little Plan A and a little Plan C.*

for students who have been on the receiving end of lots of harsh Plan A in their lives. They can escalate or shut down in the face of even just a forceful request.

There is another common misconception about the Plans that we sometimes observe after training. We might overhear an educator say to her colleague, "Oh, I already do this; everyone knows you have to pick your battles." What this educator usually means is that she is willing to drop some expectations (which is a good start!), and she thoughtfully alternates between Plan A and Plan C. However, educators that alternate between imposing will and dropping expectations are overlooking the power of the very important third option: Plan B. And you do not get Plan B by mixing a little Plan A and a little Plan C. This also comes up in classrooms with more than one educator (team teaching models, classes with a teacher and a paraprofessional, and so on), where we sometimes see what we call the *A-C split.* One adult uses mostly Plan A and the other uses mostly Plan C, in large part to compensate for the other. The Plan A educator feels like the students must be held accountable, and the Plan C educator just wants to keep the calm and not set the students off. Again, they are overlooking the power of the third option. Plan B offers an alternative that can both hold students accountable and keep the calm, rather than pursuing one at the cost of the other.

Let's cover a couple more common misconceptions about the CPS Plans. After introductory training in the Plans, people often thank us for giving them "another tool for their toolboxes." But Plan B is a process rather than a tool, and importantly, it is a process linked to a philosophy. If you decouple the "techniques" of Plan B from the mindset, the whole thing falls rather flat, and the plans won't work very well for you. As you will see in the next chapter, Plan B is hard work and if it used simply as a technique you will likely drop it if it doesn't produce immediate results. You only hang in there through the tough work of Plan B when you understand that you are building a helping relationship and building skills with a student—a student who is doing as well as he can with the skills he has!

### Plan B saves more time than it takes.

Finally, the most valuable and scarce commodity in schools is surely time, which is why we frequently hear people tell us: "I love Plan B . . . *but* I don't have time for it." We are all too familiar with how strapped for time educators are these days, trying to pack more and more content into less and less time, and get every student to the same place regardless of where they started. In this context, it is imperative to remember that the number one reason educators depart from teaching the curriculum is attending to behavioral disruptions in the classroom, a leading cause of teacher stress is behavioral challenges in the classroom. In addition, and a leading reason talented young educators drop out of the profession: you guessed it—dealing with behavioral challenges (Abel & Sewell, 1999; Boyle et al., 1995). Durably solving problems that routinely lead to behavioral disruptions always takes less time in the long run than contending with those problems again and again. Plan B saves more time than it takes.

## BEHAVIOR INTERVENTION PLANNING MADE SIMPLE

Now that you've completed the three lists on your CPS-APT, and we've introduced you to the three Plans and the goals they pursue and helped make sure you don't fall prey to common misconceptions about them, we can review how to create a CPS-friendly Behavior Intervention Plan (BIP). Thanks to the simple heuristic of the Plans, it is actually as easy as one, two, three . . . as in three options. Go back to your CPS-APT and you will notice a skinny column all the way on the left next to your list of Problems. That is where you assign a letter (A, B, or C) to each and every one of the Problems you identified, to indicate which Plan you will use for that Problem (see Box 5.4). Since your list of Problems is a list of predictable situations waiting to happen, the worst time to decide how to handle them is right when they are happening. That list gives you the luxury of deciding in a planful way, and this is where simplicity helps: You have only three options.

Start by deciding which problems you will use Plan B for first. If you have a good collaborative relationship with the student in question and the student has some skill to tolerate distress, you can choose a harder problem to solve. If, however, your relationship with the student is strained (often the case with challenging students) or the student has low stress tolerance (also often the case with challenging students), you should start with something easier—or what we call the lower-hanging fruit on your list of Problems. What qualifies as an easier Problem? Either something that you feel inherently flexible about and you're not terribly invested in the outcome and/or something that the student cares about.

Some important advice: We rarely find we wish we had started with a harder problem to solve, but we often think it would have been better to cut our Plan B teeth together on something easy in the beginning. Easier problems allow you to create a track record and have you and the student feeling good about the process and eager to try it again with other problems.

| | PROBLEMS<br>The situations WHEN the child has difficulty. Also known as expectations, precipitants, antecedents, triggers or contexts that can lead to challenging behavior. When making your list, describe the who, what, when and where and be specific! | SKILL STRUC'<br>The reasons handling this list of problen the list of the problems the skill struggles |
|---|---|---|
| **BOX 5.4. ASSIGN A PLAN FOR EACH PROBLEM TO BE SOLVED ON YOUR CPS-APT.** | | |
| Plan A, B, Or C | | |
| B | Transitioning from hall to class | Planning organizi |
| A | Bringing materials home to do homework | Keeping Shiftin( arousal |
| C | Handing in homework | Understar impact ha |

Once you decide which Problem(s) will first be assigned Plan B, a good BIP means also deciding what to do in the meantime with the other Problems on your list. Again, this is where simplicity helps! If you aren't using Plan B for a particular problem yet, you only have two other options—Plan A and Plan C. How do you decide which Plan to use? Remember our discussion earlier about the goals each Plan pursues. Plan A will attempt to get your expectation met. Plan C will reduce challenging behavior, but neither Plan A nor Plan C will solve the problem or build skills or relationship. So as a team, you have to decide what's more important to you in the meantime—pursuing your expectation even if the student escalates, or keeping the student calm even if you aren't pursuing your expectation. With a younger student, that may mean deciding whether you want to try to make her sit still on the rug during circle time even if she disrupts the rest of the class (Plan A) or you want to keep her calm and avoid the disruption to other students by letting her skip circle time or sit somewhere else (Plan C). For an older student, this might mean giving him detention if he doesn't turn in his homework again, even if he escalates and it alienates him (Plan A) or avoiding the escalation and alienation by telling him that you'll not expect the homework for now, until you have made a plan together (Plan C).

These decisions of which Plan to use for each Problem on your list should be made by consensus with the rest of the team. If they aren't, here's what will happen: Some of your colleagues will go out and do Plan A and others Plan C, creating a rift between staff. This may leave some feeling undermined, or at least as if they are working at cross-purposes. Fortunately, the three plans simplify the BIP process, helping the team come to an agreement in fairly short order during a team meeting. The CPS-APT is not intended, however, to be a laminated document that, once completed, goes untouched. It should be a living, breathing document. As you implement the BIP with the student, it should be updated and revised. You will cross off Problems that have been solved and move on to assign Plan B to others. And you will cross off certain skills that you have decided are less important, adding others that make themselves clearer over time.

Note that a common misstep is to use the Plans to prioritize the Challenging Behaviors instead of the Problems. The issue with that is that any unsafe behavior would of course lead to suggesting the use of Plan A. However, if you have identified the predictable antecedent to the unsafe behavior, you actually have all three options available to you. You could instead choose to use Plan C to remove the trigger so the challenging behavior never occurs, or Plan B to try to solve the problem that leads to the unsafe behavior in the first place. To remind you that you solve Problems and not Challenging Behaviors, you'll notice that we carefully placed the column for plans on the CPS-APT immediately next to your list of Problems.

Now that you've completed your BIP for the student, it is time to get started doing Plan B. In the next chapter, we will review the steps of Plan B. We will keep it simple by teaching you a process with only three steps. But there is a lot packed into each one of those steps.

## PART 2

# COLLABORATIVE PROBLEM SOLVING

# CHAPTER 6
## PLAN B: EMPATHIZE, SHARE, COLLABORATE

*"In our school, I mean, we actually, like, we switched up our discipline, like, a lot. Since the older way we used to do discipline, was like, we had a room. And there would be like, detention, but you'll be in there for the whole day depending on what you did. You could have talked back to the teacher the wrong way. You could have got into a fight, any of that. But . . . teachers felt like that didn't help nobody in the long run. So they got rid of that. And now it's like, you argue with a teacher it's more like you go to her and you talk to her. She'll ask you, like, why you do this? Or, like, what's the reason that you took this course of action? And it's more like that now. So, like, it's actually, completely, I feel like it's more active to get at what's wrong than, like, be like, 'Oh you're suspended. You're getting detention. You're going. You're not coming back to my class for like a week or so.' It makes us feel like we're actually being treated like students and not like little hoodlums or whatnot."*

—A high school student in New York City
whose school implemented CPS

Now that we've reviewed the different options for handling unmet expectations or problems (Plans A, B, and C) and what each option accomplishes, let's discuss the most important option: Plan B. Remember, Plan B will work on the same goals as Plan A (attempt to get your expectation met) and Plan C (decrease challenging behavior), but Plan B also works on the other three goals that neither of the other two options addresses:

1. Solve chronic problems so they don't keep occurring.
2. Build skills (and thus confidence and internal drive).
3. Build, or restore, a helping relationship.

Knowing that Plan B can help work on all those goals at once is exciting, but of course Plan B is not magic. As you begin to try Plan B with your students, keep in mind that, just as learning disabilities do not disappear overnight, Plan B takes lots of repetition—you can't rush skill development. Learning a new skill can be daunting, and practicing frequently is a crucial step in truly acquiring the skill. By prioritizing certain problems, rather than trying to solve all the problems at the same time, we are ensuring that the child can learn the skills in increments, much as we do with an academic learning disability.

## EMERGENCY PLAN B VS. PROACTIVE PLAN B

The first thing to know about Plan B is that there are actually two different types of Plan B, and the difference between them—timing—is crucial. *Emergency Plan B* (Greene, 2005; Greene & Ablon, 2005) occurs right in the midst of challenging behavior happening yet again. For example, you have a student who is, once again, not settling down to do classwork and thus disrupting other students. Emergency Plan B would be an attempt to solve that chronic problem right when it is happening. This is most challenging when the problem occurs in front other students or during instructional time, or if the problem can result in aggressive or dangerous behavior. If a student often gets into shoving matches while in line transitioning from one class or activity to another, the worst time to try to solve that problem of transitions is when it's already happening— i.e., when all the kids are lined up and the shoving and pushing has already begun. The problem with Emergency Plan B is you are on the spot, often with all eyes on you, and with a frustrated student in front of you. And if the frustrated student produces a frustrated educator, we have two frustrated people who are not at their best trying to solve a problem. No wonder Emergency Plan B doesn't tend to solve chronic problems so they don't keep coming up. Instead, Emergency Plan B can be used simply to de-escalate things or manage a crisis. But the problem will be back. So, Emergency Plan B will be there if you need it, and we'll discuss it in more detail later in this chapter. But *Proactive Plan B* is the preferred approach.

Proactive Plan B (Greene, 2005; Greene & Ablon, 2005) takes place well *before* a challenging behavior recurs. Because of this, even before you sit down to talk to the student, you can think and plan and catch the student at an opportune moment when she is calm and available—and so are you. There is nothing like a prepared educator and calm student to maximize your chance of solving a tough problem. So in the above-mentioned example, you would want to have a Proactive Plan B discussion with the student long before the next time she is supposed to line up for a transition.

## THE STEPS OF PLAN B

Whether it's Emergency Plan B or the far more preferable Proactive Plan B, the process for Plan B only has three steps (see Box 6.1), which makes it seem pretty simple. In one sense, it is. On the other hand, like any recipe with only three ingredients, if you leave one out, add one too soon, or put them in the wrong order, the result won't be optimal.

---

**BOX 6.1. THE THREE STEPS OF PLAN B.**

1. **EMPATHIZE:** Clarify the student's concern.

2. **SHARE** your concern.

3. **COLLABORATE:** Brainstorm, assess and choose a solution.

### Step #1: Empathize

The goal of this first step is to understand the student's concern or perspective about the specific Problem you've chosen to discuss. Proactive Plan B begins with a neutral observation aimed at bringing up the problem or issue without putting the student on the defensive immediately. Unfortunately when educators approach students, particularly students with a history of challenging behavior, and say they want to talk about something, most students immediately think: "I'm in trouble. What did I do?!" And most challenging students are expecting Plan A to follow pretty quickly. So you'll probably need to go overboard, especially in the beginning, to show the student that you are just hoping to understand their concerns or perspective, not to dole out punishment.

We suggest you start with something neutral, like *"I've noticed . . ."* or *"It seems like . . ."* followed by your observation of the Problem situation. It is crucial, though, that the observation is not blaming or accusing and does not assume anything. You might say: "It seems like it's been tough for you to get to class on time lately," or "It looks like lining up hasn't been going so well lately." Notice how those observations aren't about the challenging behavior we want to stop (e.g., "It looks like you've been pushing people in line lately.") and they don't make assumptions either (e.g., "It seems like you don't care about being on time for class lately.") Anything that puts the student on the defensive—such as feeling criticized or blamed—will likely result in the student refusing to participate or offering a defense, which will make the problem difficult, if not impossible, to solve. Once you have made the neutral observation, ask the student to tell you his or her perspective. This is typically accomplished by saying something like "Can you fill me in?" "Tell me about that," or "I'm just wondering what's going on."

After your neutral statement and inquiry, your next step depends on what, if anything, the student does. The student may give you useful information, or no information. The student might say, "I don't know," or look at you blankly. There are four tools you can use to gather informa-

**BOX 6.2. TOOLS FOR DRILLING DOWN DURING STEP #1.**

**1. Clarifying Questions**

These are used to get the ball rolling. They should be open-ended: How so? What's going on? Can you say more about that part? What am I not getting? What happened when you said that?

**2. Educated Guesses**

These are used when your questions aren't getting you anywhere. You can guess straight out, or you can play 20 Questions or Hot and Cold. Some examples: Mind if I take a guess? Other kids might be concerned about . . . Let me know if I'm getting warm. You're not the first kid to have this issue; can I tell you what some other kids have said?

**3. Reflective Listening**

This is used to clarify what you've learned earlier. You might say: Am I right that . . .? What I hear you saying is . . . Let's see if I've got this straight . . . It sounds like you're saying . . .

**4. Reassurance**

This is used to calm a student who may be getting upset or shutting down, or if you think that may happen. Try: You are not in trouble. I'm not saying you have to do it, I just want to understand. I know there must be an important reason this is happening. I know you're trying hard. I really want your opinion, not what you think I want you to say.

tion about the student's concern or perspective, if you don't get it right away. They are in Box 6.2.

The process of gathering information to understand the student's concern or perspective as specifically as possible isn't easy sometimes, but you won't go wrong if you stick to these four tools. If you depart from these tools, however, you'll likely find yourself back in Plan A! Why is that? Because if we are having a hard time identifying a student's concerns, chances are we will revert to talking about our own concerns. Thus, we are likely to end up with a solution that addresses our concerns but not the student's.

As hard as it is, it is very important not to rush this first step. We liken the process of Plan B to painting a room. While you might be very anxious to jump to the end, if you don't slow down and put the prep work in, the finished product won't turn out well. It's not necessarily fun to move the furniture out, lay down the dropcloth, tape the edges, sand the walls, and so on, but that's the dirty work that makes things go very smoothly when it comes time to start finally painting. The process of Plan B works the same way. You'll find that coming up with solutions to problems together with students is the easy part if you put in the hard prep work of asking clarifying questions and making educated guesses. Most of your time, in fact, will be spent in laying the groundwork for good, durable solutions to problems. We adults tend to rush to solutions. So, you may have to work hard on biting your tongue on potential solutions to a problem until you get through the work of soliciting the student's perspective.

Like a detective on an information-gathering mission, make sure you are curious and open to surprises. We are constantly impressed by how often we end up being surprised by a student's concerns or perspective. For instance, in one case, an educator discovered that a high schooler who insisted on signing up for all honors classes against his teachers' recommendations wasn't making this demand because he thought he was smarter than everyone else or because of parental pressure, but because he wanted to be with the "nerdy kids," whom he guessed would be nicer than the "bullies" he encountered in his current classes. In another case, a student whose body odor was driving away his classmates was, in fact, taking showers, using deodorant, and wearing clean clothes, but when asked in a curious, neutral way, told his teacher that he wasn't using soap in the shower because he didn't want soap that other people had used touching his body. We would never have known these concerns without asking, and doing lots of probing using our four tools! That's not to say that all concerns are very hard to identify. It is possible that the reason a student throws equipment in the locker room after basketball games is simply because he was frustrated by losing the game. Sometimes you'll need to do lots of digging, and at other times the concern will be right there on the surface for you. A student's skill at articulating concerns, needs, and thoughts will have a lot to do with how easy or hard the information-gathering process will be, as will their level of trust in you and the process.

An important tip to keep in mind while gathering information is that you are on the hunt for the student's concern, and not for her suggested solution to the problem. For example, let's imagine that the school nurse, Ms. Huntington, who has been trained in CPS, sits down with Naomi for a Proactive Plan B conversation, and starts by saying: "Naomi, I notice that you haven't been coming for your medication this week. Can you fill me in?" Naomi's response may be: "I'm not taking my medication at school!" But this is Naomi's proposed solution; it doesn't get at her concern. Ms. Huntington will only solve the problem once she understands the concern that led to that solution. So she would then use the four tools to gather information, to understand the reason Naomi is not arriving to take her medicine at school. Maybe Naomi will say: "I don't want to take it in front of everyone and have them think I'm some kind of freak." That is a concern that we can address with a flexible solution; for instance, by finding a way for Naomi to take her medications more discreetly. Maybe Naomi will say, "I'm supposed to take it with food, but I don't eat lunch because I hate the food in our cafeteria." As you can see, behind even the worst solutions (for example, skipping medication) can be very reasonable concerns, and getting specific concerns will lead us to useful solutions.

What do you do if the student doesn't have a concern? Sometimes we can get unnecessarily stuck on the word *concern;* when the student doesn't appear to have a concern, he usually still has a perspective about the problem or a reason the situation is difficult for him. Let's imagine you're trying to gather information to get a student's concern about smoking pot before class, but the student looks confused and says he doesn't have a concern. In other words, he doesn't see it as a problem. Don't forget—empathizing means understanding, not taking a position on whether this is a problem or not. Your job is still to use those four tools to gather information and understand his perspective as clearly as possible. Look again at the list of tools in Box 6.2 and consider how you might respond in this case. One idea: "Don't worry, you're not in trouble, I just want to understand (*reassurance*). So you're saying using pot at school doesn't cause any problems for you (*reflective listening*). Does it do anything for you at all (*clarifying question*)? I know other kids who say it actually helps them concentrate. Is that true for you (*educated guess*)?"

As you can see, the information-gathering process basically involves toggling back and forth among the four tools until you've gotten enough information so that you feel you sufficiently understand the student's concern or perspective. You might ask a clarifying question first. If you get information, reflect what you've heard and ask another clarifying question. If you don't get any information, reassure the student and then go back to asking questions. If that *still* doesn't work, try some educated guessing. If the student gets dysregulated during this process, the tools to use are reflective listening and reassurance. And so on. Here's a more detailed example of what that might sound like. Notice how the teacher sticks to the four tools and eventually identifies the student's concern:

> MRS. AMANI: I've noticed you've been drawing on your desk during class sometimes (*neutral observation*). Can you tell me about that (*inquiry*)?
>
> MICHAEL: I don't know.
>
> MRS. AMANI: Well, think about it for a bit. Don't worry, I'm not upset. I'm sure there must be an important reason why (*reassurance*).
>
> MICHAEL: Not really.
>
> MRS. AMANI: You're not in trouble. I just want to understand (*more reassurance*).
>
> MICHAEL: I'll stop doing it, okay?
>
> MRS. AMANI: Well, I don't want you to just stop without us knowing why you were doing it. Are you bored in class (*reassurance, then an educated guess*)?
>
> MICHAEL: I don't know.
>
> MRS. AMANI: Or do you just like to draw (*educated guess*)?
>
> MICHAEL: Not really.
>
> MRS. AMANI: So, you don't particularly like to draw (*reflective listening*).
>
> MICHAEL: Not really.
>
> MRS. AMANI: Huh. Okay. Well, that's interesting. So, you don't like to draw, but you're drawing on the desk a lot in class. I wonder why (*more reflective listening and a clarifying question*)?
>
> MICHAEL: I said I don't know!

MRS. AMANI: Remember, you're not in trouble. Really. Does drawing help you somehow in class (*reassurance and an educated guess*)?

MICHAEL: I guess so.

MRS. AMANI: How so (*clarifying question*)?

MICHAEL: It helps me think better, I guess.

MRS. AMANI: So it sounds like having something to do with your hands, like drawing, helps you think better or concentrate (*reflective listening*)?

MICHAEL: Yeah. I think so.

It may not have come easily, but with a little perseverance, Mrs. Amani uncovered Michael's concern. Many people would start offering suggestions for how to solve the problem, now that we understand the student's concern. However, there are some very important reasons not to jump to solutions. The second step, while usually quicker than the first, is important too! And remember that one of our goals is building the student's skills, and solving the problem *for* Michael will not be the best way to build his skills!

So how do you know when you are ready to move on from the first to the second step in Plan B? You are ready to move on when you have a good sense of the student's specific concern(s) or perspective(s) or what is hard for them about the Problem and can imagine that some solutions might be possible. Another good sign that you are ready to move on is that you've learned something new through the discussion—you may have had an "aha!" moment of sorts. And what if you move on prematurely? You'll be back! Your solution will be unlikely to work, and you'll need to return to the drawing board to get more information about the student's concern. In the example above, once Mrs. Amani understands that Michael is drawing on his desk in order to help him concentrate, she has had an "aha!" moment and can imagine some solutions that could work. Therefore, she is ready to move on to the second step of Plan B. The second step will almost always be dysregulating, so make sure the student is reasonably calm before proceeding.

### Step #2: Share the Adult Concern

A Problem only exists when there are two sets of apparently competing concerns about a situation. Thus, once we have a clear understanding of the student's concern/perspective, the next step is to ensure that the adult's concern is expressed as well. This is important for several reasons. First, students may truly not know why the expectation or situation is important to the adult. Second, taking others' perspective is often a skill that students lack. If the student has been heard during the first step of Plan B, then she is more likely to hear the adult's concern and thus practice this vital perspective-taking skill, having just had it modeled for her first.

The good news about the second step is that when planning a Proactive Plan B conversation, you can prepare before talking to the student by asking yourself: "What is my true concern?" "Why do I want her to act differently?" "Is my concern realistic?" With the example above, Mrs. Amani will want to ask herself before initiating the Plan B with Michael: "Why don't I want him drawing on his desk?" The obvious answer is that it is destroying property. But believe it or not, we need more information than this. The more specific our concerns the better. Why don't we want him destroying property? Because the desk belongs to everyone, and other students might not want to work on a desk that's been defaced or might find it distracting. And it makes our school look less nice. And it might mean extra work for the custodian.

How can you help yourself and your colleagues get more specific about your concerns? Most concerns that are important to adults relate to one of four categories: health, safety, learning, or how a student's behavior affects others. So if someone is struggling to clarify the adults' concerns, look in those four categories. Is it a health issue, learning issue, safety issue, or issue of how the behavior is impacting someone else (including you, by the way)? If the answer to any of these questions is yes, it's time to get more specific. The great benefit to being specific with our concerns is that the more specific the concerns are, the more possible solutions open up before our eyes.

Just as the students' solutions are different from their concerns, it is important to remember that your rules are not the same as your concerns, either! Rules, in fact, are adults' solutions to what are usually some very reasonable concerns. Why do you have a rule that students can't wear their hoods during class? Is it because you can't see their faces, which makes it hard for you to tell if they are following material you are teaching? Or is it because a hood may obscure gang bandanas? The difference is important, because it sets the stage for effective problem solving that will work for both of you. How do you express your concerns, once you identify them? Simply say something like, "My concerns is . . ." What I'm worried about is . . ." What matters to me is . . ." or "What would make me happy is . . ."

By the way, don't expect the student to wholeheartedly embrace your concern. In fact, she may tell you she doesn't care about your concern at all. Students are quick to disregard our concerns, because history tells them that when adults state their concerns, that is the signal that the student's concerns just got demoted in importance and are about to be trumped by adult concerns. So is this the point at which Plan B gets stuck in the mud? No! Remember that the student doesn't need to value your concern any more than you need to value hers! Each of you just needs to take each other's concern into consideration when it's time to make a solution. If Michael says, "I don't care about the custodian! That's his job to clean up the desks," Mrs. Amani might respond, "You don't have to care about him. But I do. What you care about is having something to do with your hands so you can concentrate in class when you get antsy. Right?"

The great news is that we are about to demonstrate how we can solve that problem without either Mrs. Amani or Michael sacrificing their concerns. We're going to let the student know that his concerns and our concerns are equally important, and we are just as invested in getting his concerns addressed as we are ours. Now onto the final step!

### Step #3: Collaborate

In this last step of Plan B, the aim is to collaborate on brainstorming solutions that address both concerns. We suggest kicking off the brainstorming with a statement that recaps both the concerns, so as to summarize the Problem that you are trying to solve. Remind the student and yourself of the concerns you are trying to reconcile. For example, "So the problem is that you like to climb up the slide, and I worry someone will get hurt if some kids are climbing up while other kids are going down. I wonder if there is a way that kids can go both up and down the slide and still have no one get hurt?"

Once the Problem is summarized, with both concerns presented, ask the student to try coming up with a solution before you suggest your own (for example, "Can you think of a way?"). This is critical, for three reasons. First, this will give you another chance to assess the student's problem-solving skills. His response will tell you a lot. He will have good ideas, bad ideas, or no ideas, and each tells you something about his current skill level. Second, while of course we want to solve the problem and reduce the challenging behavior, we also want to help the student practice the skills that are weak. Generating solutions practices many problem-solving skills. Third, in addition to assessing current skills and practicing new skills, giving the student a chance to coauthor the solutions will make it more likely that he is invested in solutions.

So does that mean you have to go with whatever solution the student suggests? Of course not! Get as many ideas on the list as possible. Then use a simple test to judge the quality of each idea: *Does it address your concern? Does it address my concern? Is it practical, considering the skills of all parties? Does it raise other concerns?* Walking a student through the process of testing out proposed solutions provides more practice at important problem-solving skills related to impulse control and planning. Of course, many students may struggle with the skill of generating alternative solutions. If they have no ideas, you can suggest a few to consider together. How does this last step look in the example we've been following?

> MRS. AMANI: I bet there's some way we can help you concentrate in class without it distracting the other kids or causing more work for the custodian. Can you think of a way?
>
> MICHAEL: I could draw in pencil instead of pen?
>
> MRS. AMANI: That's one idea. Let's think about that. Would it address your concern of having something to do with your hands to help you concentrate *(beginning to walk Michael through testing out the solution)*?

**MICHAEL:** Yup.

**MRS. AMANI:** Okay. Would that address my concern?

**MICHAEL:** Yup.

**MRS. AMANI:** Just a second. That solution would help you concentrate, but the desk would still get dirty and need to be cleaned by the custodian. And I think the kids might still be distracted by the drawings on your desk.

**MICHAEL:** Oh.

**MRS. AMANI:** Any other ideas?

**MICHAEL:** I could draw on something else.

**MRS. AMANI:** Interesting idea. Like what?

**MICHAEL:** I don't know.

**MRS. AMANI:** Well, what if you had a pad that was just for that kind of doodling—do you think you could do that?

**MICHAEL:** I guess so.

**MRS. AMANI:** It gives you something to do with your hands to help you concentrate?

**MICHAEL:** Yes.

**MRS. AMANI:** It's less likely to distract other students, and won't make a mess for the custodian, right?

**MICHAEL:** Yes.

**MRS. AMANI:** Can you think of any other reasons it wouldn't work or new problems it would bring up?

**MICHAEL:** Nope.

**MRS. AMANI:** Okay. Let's give it a try and see how it works. We can check in after a few days to see how it's going and make a different plan if we need to. Want to go find a pad now?

Who wins in this scenario? Both Michael and Mrs. Amani do. Who loses? No one. And what about the five goals we reviewed in Chapter 5? Was Mrs. Amani pursuing her expectation? Definitely. Reducing challenging behavior? Yes. Building a helping relationship? Absolutely. Solving a chronic problem so it doesn't keep coming up? Yes. And finally, was Mrs. Amani teaching Michael problem-solving skills? Again, the answer should be a resounding yes! Many of the skills we covered in Chapter

4 were modeled and practiced in these three simple steps of Plan B, including expressing thoughts and needs in words, considering the impact of one's behaviors on others, and considering multiple solutions to a problem. As you can see, the skills training is embedded in the process. While not the kind of direct skill instruction educators are used to, it has many advantages over didactic skills training. We will discuss this more in Chapter 7.

# CHAPTER 7

## TEACH SKILLS WHILE SOLVING REAL PROBLEMS

*Mrs. McConnell looks at the weekly suspension list in her hand. As the school adjustment counselor at South Elementary School for five years now, this is the most frustrating part of her job. She has been working with Teddy for months on "Stop. Think. Act." They have role-played over and over what he will do when he gets angry on the playground. Every time he leaves, she is confident that they have finally made some progress on improving his impulse control. The suspension list indicates that while she was at training on Friday, Teddy pushed another student off the monkey bars during an argument. She puts the time of Teddy's reentry meeting into her calendar, and thinks: "What more can I do?"*

When we teach educators about the skills deficits that are to blame for behavioral challenges in the classroom, we are often asked for the curriculum, workbook, or at least a list that describes all the different ways to teach those skills to the students for whom they are lagging. As disappointing as it is to hear at first, such a workbook doesn't exist. This is because we don't focus on training neurocognitive skills through direct instruction and didactics. Rather, the skills are taught through the naturalistic and relational process of solving problems together with students. If a student is struggling with certain problem-solving skills, what's the best way to help her develop better problem-solving skills? Practice a lot of problem solving with her! To do so, you will not use someone else's problems or hypothetical problems from a workbook, but rather real-life problems with real people in the student's life, including you! While the bad news is that some students present a lot of problems in your classroom, the good news is that all those problems represent naturally occurring opportunities to practice problem-solving skills. Take a look at Box 7.1 to see all the skills students practice, with our help, within each of the three steps of Plan B. If you follow the steps of Plan B, you are ensuring that these skills get practiced.

| BOX 7.1. STUDENTS PRACTICE AND BUILD SKILLS IN EACH PLAN B STEP. | |
|---|---|
| **Plan B Step** | **Skills Practiced by Students** |
| **1.** EMPATHIZE: Clarify the student's concern. | Identifying, clarifying, and expressing concerns; regulating themselves and their emotions. |
| **2.** SHARE your concern. | Perspective taking; recognizing their impact on others; empathy. |
| **3.** COLLABORATE: Brainstorm, assess, and choose solution. | Generating solutions; reflecting on multiple thoughts; considering outcomes; moving off original idea. |

This form of naturalistic skills training is actually preferable to gathering students in small "lunch bunch" or other skills groups to practice set skills through role playing and exercises. Why is that? First, most social-emotional learning programs involve direct instruction of these skills, based on the assumption that the student agrees that he needs to be taught these skills. In CPS, however, the student doesn't need to sign on to receive skills training. In fact, he doesn't even need to agree that he lacks the skill, much less that he wants you to help him develop it, in order to participate. With Plan B, all the student has to be willing to do is talk with you to solve problems in ways that work out well for him, too. The skills training happens automatically. This is very good news because we find that the most challenging students often do not feel that they need skill instruction, or they find it pointless and boring, and therefore do not engage in the lessons in a meaningful way, making it even harder for those lessons to translate to real-world skills.

The second reason that we find naturalistic skills training in Plan B to be better than didactic skills training is something called the *specificity principle of neuroplasticity*. Like Teddy, a student may look as though he is acquiring skills when you teach him about social skills or problem solving in your office or classroom, but then the skills seem to vanish when it is time to apply them out on the playground or in the lunchroom. Recent brain research suggests that to build or change a neural network, you must activate that *specific* neural network (Kleim & Jones, 2008). Unfortunately, artificial circumstances in an office or even at lunch bunch don't recruit the actual neural network that is activated when someone has to apply a skill in a real-life situation. This explains the persistent and frustrating lack of generalizability of these skills, where the skills don't transfer from the place they are practiced to the place where they need to be applied. Plan B gets around this fundamental flaw in most skills-training approaches by having students practice their skills in the real environment with the real people with whom they interact, thereby activating the actual neural networks required to demonstrate the skill.

The third benefit of this naturalistic skills training is that the adult acts as a real-world model from whom the student can learn. As long as you do the steps in the right order, the adult models many of the skills for the student first, before asking the student to try his hand at the skill. Perhaps the best example involves the social thinking skill of empathy, which many educators feel is the hardest skill to effectively train. In the first step of Plan B, the adult first models what empathy looks like by empathizing with the student's concern. Again, this is not a hypothetical form of empathy, but rather empathy for a real-life concern that resonates emotionally for the student. Recall that it is not until the adult has empathized sufficiently so that the student feels understood that they move to the second step of Plan B, which is when the adult asks the student to try what has just been modeled—namely, to empathize with the adult's concern. And if the student struggles to appreciate the adult's concern (showing difficulty empathizing), they return again to the first step of Plan B so the adult can again model what empathy looks like before proceeding to the second step and asking the student to try empathizing again. Plan B includes a powerful, repetitive process of modeling the skill and then asking the student to try it—model, practice, model, practice, model, practice.

The fourth benefit of naturalistic skills training in Plan B is that you don't have to train a single skill at a time, and the skills training is automatically individualized for each student. Plan B will go smoothly where the student has the skills to easily engage in the process, but it will be harder where the student struggles with certain skills. For example, if a student has good language and communication skills but poor perspective-taking skills, the first step ought to be easy, but the process may come to a crashing halt when you raise your concern in the second step! As a result, you and the student won't spend much time in the first step, practicing skills she doesn't need to work on, but will be forced to dig in and do the hard work right where the student needs it most. Because of this, students don't need to sit through weeks of a skills-training curriculum that aren't relevant, and you don't even need to decide which skills to target first. The Plan B process will tell you all by itself! You just need to keep an eye out for when Plan B gets tough.

For this reason, Plan B isn't just an intervention, it might also be your most potent assessment procedure. If you want to know which specific problem-solving skills a student lacks, just try problem solving with her and watch where she gets stuck! Knowing that a student is bound to get stuck where she has skills deficits also helps you resist saying: "I tried Plan B, and it didn't work!" when you don't immediately come to a durable solution. Rather, we hope that after reading this chapter you will say: "I tried Plan B, and of course it didn't solve the problem yet because we ran right into struggles with the skills that the student needs a lot of help practicing!" You would be unlikely to say: "We tried long division with him, and it didn't work!" Instead, you would realize that learning a new conceptual skill requires successive attempts with lots of struggles along the way before success becomes more consistent. The same is true for these neurocognitive skills.

The fifth benefit of naturalistic—rather than didactic—skills training is that the students aren't the only ones building skills. Unfortunately, we adults (these authors included!) all have some skill struggles, and those skill struggles can make Plan B extra tough. After all, how are we supposed to train skills if we struggle with them, too? In fact, if you practice Plan B often, you will notice a couple of patterns. You may notice a *within-student* pattern, where Plan B gets stuck consistently with the same student. That will tell you which skills that particular student needs to build the most. But you may also notice an *across-student* pattern where Plan B tends to get stuck regardless of who the student is. That particular pattern will tell you where *you* struggle the most! Fortunately, guess who else gets to practice all these same skills during every Plan B conversation? Yes, you guessed it—we do! Every time we try Plan B with a student, we are practicing skills alongside them. See Box 7.2 for examples. Again, Plan B can be a very powerful assessment tool for us as well as for our students. It confirms where we need to practice and also provides that practice.

| BOX 7.2. ADULTS PRACTICE AND BUILD SKILLS IN EACH PLAN B STEP. | |
|---|---|
| **Plan B Step** | **Skills Practiced by Adults** |
| **1.** EMPATHIZE: Clarify the student's concern. | Perspective taking; empathizing; emotion and self-regulation. |
| **2.** SHARE your concern. | Identifying, clarifying, and expressing our concerns in words. |
| **3.** COLLABORATE: Brainstorm, assess, and choose solution. | Generating solutions; reflecting on multiple thoughts; considering outcomes; moving off original idea. |

Finally, the greatest advantage to the naturalistic skills training that occurs in Plan B is that it is embedded in an empathic, relational process. Why is that important? We will explain in detail in Chapter 8, by reviewing the neurobiology behind healthy human brain development and revealing how that maps directly onto the Plan B process.

# CHAPTER 8

## HOW PLAN B CHANGES THE BRAIN

*When it is time to go get Marcus for his pull-out, Ms. Riley, the reading specialist, can tell right away that it's going to be "one of those days." First, Marcus insists that he does not need to go because he doesn't need any more help with his reading. When Ms. Riley gently tries to persuade him to leave the class and come with her to her office, Marcus begins loudly telling her that she is being unfair. Ms. Riley tries to remind him that they agreed to this plan, but Marcus won't even let her finish her sentence. He covers his ears and crouches in the back corner of the classroom, and the other students are now watching, wide-eyed. Doing her best to remain calm, Ms. Riley lets Marcus know that she can understand how he does not want to leave his friends, but she explains that he will not be missing anything particularly fun. Finally, she tells him that it is not negotiable, and he must come with her. It has become pretty clear that whatever she says, Marcus isn't listening. He has gone from 0 to 60 yet again, and Ms. Riley knows that when he is like this there is no reasoning with him.*

Fortunately, to understand the brain science behind CPS and Plan B, you don't need to have a degree in neurobiology. In fact, there are three basic concepts about brain science that capture most of what you need to know and explain why CPS is both a neurobiologically grounded and trauma-sensitive approach.

## CONCEPT 1: ACCESSING THE "SMART PART" OF A BRAIN IS CRITICAL FOR BUILDING SKILLS.

You've probably heard of the hemispheres of the human brain (are you right-brained or left-brained?), and that there are different lobes that do different things (for instance, the frontal lobe is famous for helping you plan and organize, while the temporal lobe helps you comprehend language). What you may not realize, though, is that both those concepts of hemispheres and lobes are referring just to the part of the brain that is right under your skull; that topmost, outermost, wrinkly part of the brain called the cerebral cortex (or *cortex*, for short). The cortex is the part of the brain you hear about the most because that's the part that is in charge of many of the functions of our brain that we believe make us human; like memory, awareness, thought, language, and consciousness. You might call it the "smart" part of your brain, where you do all your thinking.

Important to our conversation, however, are two other parts of the brain that lie hidden underneath the cortex (See Box 8.1). In our evolutionary history, those other two parts were earlier to develop, and they are more critical to basic survival. The midbrain, which is the closest to the spine, is in charge of very basic functions, such as heart rate, breathing, vision and hearing, motor control, arousal/alertness (including sleeping and waking), and temperature regulation. The limbic system, made of multiple parts between the spine and cortex, is known for basic emotional responses. If the cortex is the thinking part of your brain, the limbic system is the feeling and reacting part. The reason this undercarriage is important to CPS is that, like a building that needs a strong foundation, in order for a person to access the cortex for activities like recalling, planning, and reasoning, everything must be in order in the midbrain and limbic system.

If you have ever been in a car accident and tried to make decisions such as whom to call or how to best move your car to the side of the road, you may remember that access to sensible decision making was impeded by your emotional state and the degree to which your heart rate and breathing were out of control. Once those were back in order, you were in much

**BOX 8.1. THE KEY BRAIN REGIONS FOR CPS.**

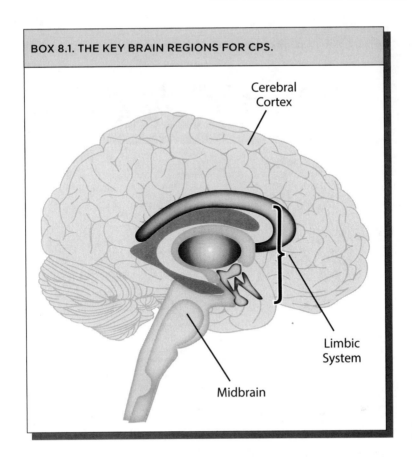

Cerebral Cortex

Limbic System

Midbrain

better shape to think and reason. A useful way to remember this neuro-biologic sequence is what neuroscientist Dr. Bruce Perry (2006) calls the three Rs of information processing: *regulate*, *relate*, then *reason* (See Box 8.2). A student must be emotionally regulated before she feels comfortable enough to relate to you; and she must relate to you before you can reason with her. Every one of us has tried to reason with a dysregulated person, with no success. It's useless to talk to the student's cortex when the cortex is offline waiting for the limbic system or midbrain to calm down.

Putting this all together, if we hope to build skills like flexibility, frustration tolerance, and problem solving in our students (skills that are all managed by the cortex), we need to help the students practice those skills in real-life situations. To practice those skills, we need to access the cortex. To get access to the cortex, we must first ensure that the students are regulated and related.

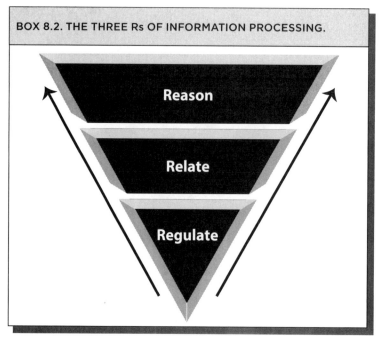

BOX 8.2. THE THREE Rs OF INFORMATION PROCESSING.

Reason

Relate

Regulate

## CONCEPT 2: STRESS AND TRAUMA AFFECT THE BRAIN.

The development of the brain is a complex and finely tuned process influenced by the interplay between genes and environment. That is, while some of how your brain develops, including the basic structure, is largely determined by your DNA, many details of development are impacted by specific events that occur prenatally, perinatally, and postnatally, and then throughout your life.

Trauma affects the brain by making connections between brain cells, or neurons, that have a negative impact on brain function. In typical human development with normal stressors, the stress response system develops in a typical and predictable way. However, if an individual experiences unpredictable, extreme, or uncontrollable stressors, the network of neurons that makes up the stress response system can get organized in an abnormal way, resulting in a domino effect of abnormal brain activity in the affected individual. Additionally, traumatic events cause the brain to make connections that are adaptive in traumatic situations but not adaptive for most everyday situations. For instance, a student with an abusive parent will become hyperaware of others' facial expressions, which may help predict violent outbursts at home, but may lead to biases toward reading other people's neutral expressions as hostile. The result of traumatic experiences, then, are actual biological differences in neural networks of the brain. These biological differences then manifest in trouble with flexibility, frustration tolerance, and problem solving. Thus, while some children have skill struggles due to biological differences that are hereditary, many others have skill struggles because of their experiences with trauma.

It is important to note here that we are referring not only to trauma in the traditional sense of the word, such as when experiencing one or more life-threatening incidents, or when facing abuse or neglect. We are also referring to trauma in the sense of being exposed to chronic overwhelming stress. This has been referred to as *toxic stress*, because it can have the same effect on brain development as toxins (Shonkoff et al., 2012). Examples of toxic stress include not knowing where your next meal is coming from, contending with high-level conflict at home, or being faced with a caretaker struggling with a substance use disorder or mental health issues. Also important to consider is that any student who strug-

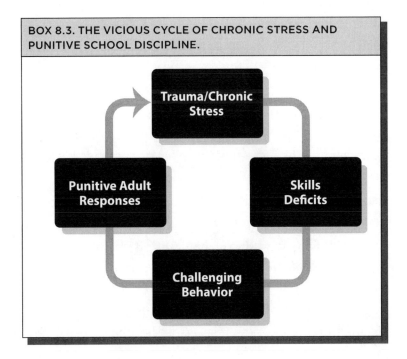

BOX 8.3. THE VICIOUS CYCLE OF CHRONIC STRESS AND PUNITIVE SCHOOL DISCIPLINE.

gles to meet the basic expectations of the school day, and is thus on the receiving end of traditional school discipline, may experience their days at school as chronically stressful. The sad irony in this case is that the relationship can be circular (See Box 8.3): A child exposed to trauma that has resulted in skills deficits exhibits challenging behavior when she cannot meet adult expectations, and adult responses to that behavior create additional chronic overwhelming stress, and further impact skill deficits.

## CONCEPT 3: BRAINS CAN CHANGE.

The bad news, as described above, is that brain development can be delayed or arrested due to chronic stress and trauma. The good news is that, contrary to the commonly held belief that you can't teach an old dog (or person!) new tricks, science has recently revealed that the brain stays malleable to a greater degree and for much longer than we thought. It is true that there are particular periods in our lives (such as infancy and adolescence) when our brains are particularly sensitive to certain types of input and learning; however, it's never too late to learn something new and to build skills.

When we learn, we strengthen connections between certain areas of the brain that hadn't been connected before, or that weren't connected as strongly as others. Have you ever gone out after a big snowstorm and tried to carve a new path in the snow with a sled? The first time you do it, it's tough going. Then, as you go down that same path many more times, the path gets smoother and your trips become more efficient and effortless. Your neural networks, the system of connections between your brain cells, are like a web of these paths, some well worn and some barely traveled. Those that have been "ridden" the most are the ones that are most efficient and effortless.

Much as you can only work on smoothing your sled's path by traveling down that path over and over, to change a neural pathway you need to engage that specific pathway repetitively as well. Those who treat phobias will tell you that if you want to learn to better tolerate spiders, you must activate the part of your brain that gets upset when seeing a spider, and then practice a new response. The challenge, when working with traumatized youth, is to activate the stress response safely. When a child is faced with small, predictable amounts of stress, it is considered good stress that challenges the child to grow and learn. Thus, we want to create learning opportunities for our students, but the key is finding the right dose and spacing for the stress we deliver. If you deliver too much stress, the student may become dysregulated, and learning can't occur. If you deliver too little stress, it may not be enough to activate the stress response, and learning can't occur. If the dose is appropriate, but is applied constantly, with no space between doses, the neural network becomes unresponsive, and learning can't occur. Thus, brain change depends upon activating the right neural network, and repeatedly applying moderate doses of stress with space in between.

## WHAT DO THESE BRAIN CONCEPTS TELL US ABOUT PLAN B?

Let's review the three brain concepts covered in this chapter, and then consider what they might have to do with the Collaborative Problem Solving approach:

1.  Accessing the "smart" part of the brain (called the cortex) is critical for building skills; and to do so, the brain must first be regulated and related.
2.  Difficulties with flexibility, frustration tolerance, and problem-solving reflect differences in the brain. In some cases, those differences are caused by chronic stress and trauma, which can arrest brain development.
3.  Brains can change when exposed to moderate, predictable patterns of stress.

As we discussed in Chapter 7, many of your most challenging students struggle with their emotion-regulation skills. Dysregulated students are those who get really worked up really fast and/or can't control a strong emotional response. Whether due to traumatic experiences, chronic stress, or heredity, they may become so flooded with emotion that they aren't able to think straight. Now you know why a dysregulated person is never in a great position to think or learn new skills. Thus, you must make sure to regulate a student before you can begin to speak to the smart part of his brain (cortex) in a way to promote learning. This means you need to be careful not to use top-down, or cortex-first, approaches to build skills with students who are easily dysregulated. They won't be able to do it! In order to access the smart part of the brain to build skills, you must start low down in the brain, and work your way up through the midbrain and the limbic system, before finally gaining access to the wonderful thinking machine we call the cortex. Good news: You already know how! Just follow the three steps of Plan B in the order that we taught you (Perry & Ablon, 2014; see Box 8.4).

**STEP 1—REGULATE** The first step of Plan B (when you empathize with the child's concern) is the regulating step. Being heard and having her perspective understood is regulating, and you help regulate the student by using reflective listening and reassurance to reach the midbrain. Recall that you only use the other information-gathering tools in the first step to understand the student's concern or perspective when she is regulated enough to help provide that information. After maintaining, or regaining, regulation, and when you understand the student's concern, it is time to move to the second step of Plan B.

**STEP 2—RELATE** During the second step of Plan B (sharing your concern), you have moved up the brain and are doing relational activity, by putting two sets of concerns on the balance, and practicing taking each other's perspective to understand the other's concern. If (or more likely *when*) the student becomes dysregulated upon hearing your concern, it's time to go back to regulate that midbrain; you retreat to the first step. This brings you right back down to the bottom of the brain to reregulate the student before proceeding to try sharing your concern again as you move up to the limbic region.

**STEP 3—REASON** Once you and the regulated student are relating to one another and understanding each other's concerns, only then

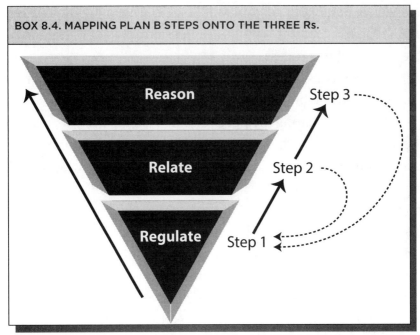

BOX 8.4. MAPPING PLAN B STEPS ONTO THE THREE Rs.

do you move to the third step and ask the student to collaborate with you to brainstorm solutions. In the third step, you are inviting the student's cortex to come to the table. Since you've ensured that the foundation is sturdy, you are ready to try engaging the top of the brain. If at any point in the process, even once your cortexes are trying to create a solution together, the student gets dysregulated, you simply revert back to the first step and repeat the process, working from the bottom up.

If it seems to you that honoring this neurobiologic sequence of "regulate, relate, reason" to access the smart part of the brain for problem solving is going to require a lot of repetition and many small bursts of stress for the student, you are right. As mentioned before, brain change depends upon repeatedly applying moderated doses of stress to the right neural network, with time in between. Fortunately Plan B is by nature repetitive; in that most problems require more than one Plan B conversation, there are multiple repetitions of skill practice imbedded in each conversation, and you will parry back and forth between the steps of Plan B to keep the student regulated and related before reasoning. While the repetitive nature of Plan B may at first feel frustrating, we encourage you to recognize that this revisiting of the steps of Plan B is at the heart of the skill-building process.

Plan B is also designed to be moderately stressful. While the first step of Plan B is meant to be regulating, the second step is almost always dysregulating. Adults sharing their concerns is dysregulating because most students have learned that teachers' concerns tend to trump students' concerns. But remember that this dysregulation is not necessarily a bad thing. This is the small dose of good stress that is needed to build new connections in the brain. Also, if the problem-solving process always went quickly and smoothly (i.e., not much stress), the student probably didn't need much practice with problem-solving skills and didn't learn much! Plan B will get stuck in specific places that will stretch the skills of the student (and perhaps yours also). By repeatedly taking a student down the path of Plan B, you are providing the student with the manageable, predictable doses of good stress that will promote brain change. After repeated doses, that path gets worn smooth like the well-traveled sled path, making it more likely that the student will be able to effectively and efficiently travel down that path to solve problems on his own in the future.

After learning these fundamental concepts of brain change, you may suddenly find yourself skeptical of the methods by which we typically deliver school discipline and social-emotional skill building, and you are right. While we are less likely today to send a student to the principal's office for misbehavior, we still often outsource the discipline and social-emotional skill building to the school psychologist or guidance counselor. A challenging student may be given a 20-minute opportunity twice a week on the grid to focus on skill building. But the brain doesn't change only from 1:20 to 1:40 on Tuesdays and Thursdays, and it is unlikely to change very much at all with such sporadic dosing. Classroom teachers and aides/paraprofessionals are the ideal individuals who can provide the number of doses required to change the brain.

So how else do you ensure that the stress you cause is moderate, predictable, and controlled? There are many ways to achieve this using CPS. First, picking the right problem to start with is important. Aim for a problem that will cause enough stress to promote learning, but not so much to cause severe dysregulation. Second, you have a predictable process in Plan B that the students learn to expect. Plan B is comprised of the same three steps in the same order each time. Third, if the dose becomes too intense, you return to the regulating steps of Plan B. If it is still too intense, you can default to Plan C, and return to the problem later, knowing that you supplied one dose. Fourth, provide just enough assistance with the parts of Plan B with which the student struggles. If you do too much work for the student, she won't be stressed enough to learn. On the other hand, if you leave her to her own devices and she lacks the skill to solve problems effectively, it will be too stressful. Developmental psychologist, Lev Vygotsky (1930-1934/1978), long ago talked about the zones of proximal development, from which the notion of scaffolding grew. Scaffolding in Plan B is crucial.

## MORE ON CPS AND TRAUMA

An overwhelming majority of students who are frequently the targets of school discipline are the students who have been affected by chronic stress and trauma. As an educator, being trauma-sensitive means recognizing that challenging behavior is a peripheral effect of skill struggles, which themselves are due to differences in brain development, sometimes as a result of chronic overwhelming stress and trauma.

With students who have histories of chronic stress and trauma, scaffolding is particularly important. Traumatized students are likely to get triggered by Plan B itself, particularly students who have good reason to fear an adult trying to achieve some relational intimacy with them. For many traumatized students, there are well-worn pathways in the brain connecting relational intimacy and fear. For this reason, Plan B itself, even with an empathic educator, can be a trigger. Titrating the amount of stress via dosing and spacing is never as important as for a traumatized student. Just asking about their concerns or perspectives may feel dysregulating and might be too much of a dose. This is, again, where Plan B provides a helpful structure. You do not proceed to the second step of Plan B if the student becomes dysregulated. Rather, you do your best to re-regulate her with reassurance and reflection, and if need be, stop the process. That may be the tiny dose that is all that particular student can handle for now. Over time, you learn to negotiate together with the student how much of a dose he can handle. By doing so, you are trying to create new connections in the brain, to forge a pathway from relational intimacy to collaboration and problem solving, as opposed to panic and alert.

Besides allowing you to moderate the dose of stress you deliver, there are other ways in which CPS is considered a trauma-sensitive approach to school discipline. In recent years, our understanding of how to help traumatized students has begun to de-emphasize methods of reprocessing trauma, as doing so is thought to strengthen existing associations in the brain created by the trauma. Also, while we have learned you cannot erase old associations in the brain, we have learned that trauma-sensitive care can create new connections in the brain. This is done by helping students to confront triggering situations safely, to slowly desensitize them over time, using the Plan B process. With traumatized students, we aim to avoid the use of power and control (Plan A), which is thought to be re-traumatizing and to cause developmental damage. On the contrary, we attempt to reduce the power differential. Allowing the student's concerns to be as important as the educator's effectively reduces that power differential without the educator losing any authority. Traumatized students are often desperate for control; however, having sole responsibility can be overwhelming for them. During Plan B, the student is coauthor of solutions, but is not on his own. Traditional school discipline relies heavily on mechanisms of power and control to try to manipulate students' behavior, which runs counter to these principles of trauma-sensitive teaching, as well as what we know about how the brain works. Thankfully, most schools and districts now recognize the importance of being trauma-sensitive, however they still often struggle to know how to make that information actionable. CPS can be an effective way to help bring this knowledge into practice. Even better, using trauma-sensitive discipline helps all students build skills, not just those who have endured chronic stress and trauma. CPS helps teachers keep in mind what we know about how *all* students' brains process information and build skills.

# CHAPTER 9
## PRACTICE, PRACTICE, PRACTICE: PLANNING AND TROUBLESHOOTING PLAN B

> *After yet another blow-up with Marcus, Ms. Riley returns to the quiet of her office, closes the door, and breathes deeply. There has to be a better way to reach Marcus so they don't keep repeating this pattern every Tuesday afternoon. The time she spends just trying to get Marcus to come to her office would be better spent using the multi-sensory reading approach in which Ms. Riley has been trained. Clearly the worst time to try to solve this problem is right in the heat of the moment when Marcus is refusing to attend and is having a meltdown. Perhaps if she can pick a good time outside the moment to talk with Marcus about the problem, and come up with a way to bring it up that doesn't trigger him, the conversation might go better . . .*

In Chapter 6, we discussed how Proactive Plan B is the preferable form, because you can catch the student when he is calm and accessible *and* you have had some time to think and prepare. In this chapter, we will describe how to prepare for a Proactive Plan B conversation, as well as how to troubleshoot afterward when it doesn't go smoothly. When you are new to Plan B, doing this kind of advance preparation will make things much easier. Think of it like the training wheels used when learning how to ride a bike. Ultimately, the goal is to be able to do Plan B frequently without necessarily having to prepare each step in advance. If you had to prepare every Plan B discussion, it is unlikely you could achieve the frequency of dosing required to change the brain that we described in the previous chapter. Rest assured that once you practice enough Plan B and develop a natural rhythm, you won't need to formulate it in advance.

The first consideration when preparing for Plan B is *who* should be leading the conversation with the student. This is not a simple question. We mentioned in Chapter 8 how one of the remnants of conventional school discipline is that we tend to outsource school discipline by sending the student to someone else to solve a problem that happened in the classroom. We used to send the student to the principal or vice principal. Now, in many places, it may be the guidance counselor or the school psychologist whose door is left open, waiting for students to be sent from the classroom. However, the ideal person to have a Plan B conversation is the adult closest to the problem, because this adult understands the context of the problem, can articulate his or her concern specifically, will be there next time around to enact the solution, and will have repeated opportunities to practice the process together with the student.

The challenge is that the adult closest to the problem often has a strained relationship with the student because of problems like this. Another practical consideration is that, unfortunately, classroom teachers are often the ones who get the least training in a practice like CPS since it is hard to remove them from the classroom for intensive professional development. So, in an ideal world, the best person to do Plan B is an adult close to the problem who has both a good relationship with the student as well as familiarity and expertise with Plan B. Unfortunately, our experience is that those three qualities are rarely embodied in a single adult at school. The solution, then, is to tag team. Perhaps the guidance counselor who has had more training and has a better relationship with the student at this time (by virtue of not having to pursue the same expectations as the classroom teacher) teams up with the teacher who is close to the problem to have a Plan B conversation. Incidentally, this is also a great way for teachers and other school staff to share the process of learning Plan B alongside each other. People often worry that having two adults doing Plan B with one student will lead to the student feeling ganged up on. In our experience, however, contrary to when two adults are using Plan A at once, when two educators are using Plan B, and are working really hard to understand and address the student's concern, it actually feels doubly good to students.

Once you have selected who will be doing Plan B, you can think about other practical implications, such as *when* and *where* and *while doing what* you will have the conversation. Some Plan B conversations require some measure of privacy, while others can be done right there in the classroom while other students are occupied in their learning. Since time is always an issue at school, you will want to be thoughtful about when you can carve out a few minutes to have a Plan B conversation. It is important to note here that Plan B is a problem-solving conversation, not a therapy session. That is, it is not 50 minutes long! The average Plan B conversation takes between five and 10 minutes. Wherever you might find five to 10 minutes to talk to an individual student about any academic challenge she may be having, that is time in which you can carve out the time for Plan B. Remember that Proactive Plan B will save you lots of time currently spent contending with the recurrent behavioral issue. You might choose lunchtime, during recess, ask the student to come in a few minutes early or to stay after school, or potentially use a free period. Finding the time to do Plan B amid the hectic pace of the school is not easy, but it is critical.

As we discussed in Chapter 6, most students are immediately defensive when an adult in a position of power in a school asks to talk to them. Thus, you will want to do anything you can to keep the student regulated during the conversation. For this reason, sitting across a desk and staring a student in the eye during Plan B may not be such a great idea. Consider taking a walk around the building, having a snack, shooting a basketball, or even just making sure that the student has a fidget toy as you talk. Giving thought to the student's preference for eye contact or lack thereof, as well as her general comfort in the conversation, is important. One vice principal with whom we worked initially insisted that students sit up straight, look her in the eye, and stop fidgeting when attempting Plan B conversations. Ironically, all those attempts to have serious, focused conversations backfired with her most dysregulated students, who incidentally were always the ones coming to her office because of behavioral issues! We remember how different her office looked when school started the next fall. She had a beanbag chair and lots of fidget toys at the ready.

Having decided who will have the conversation, when, where, and while doing what, you can then plan some of the specifics of the steps of Plan B. The first thing to plan is how you will kick off the conversation. Recall that the first step of Plan B starts with a neutral observation. When new at this, you should literally write down what your opening line will be so that you are able to craft it in the way that is least likely to dysregulate the student. If, while looking back at your CPS-APT, you recall that the student struggles with language and communication skills, you will also want to brainstorm what types of questions you might ask, and what types of educated guesses you might make to get to the bottom of what his concern might be. Be careful to lead the student as little as possible, but some students will require a fair amount of scaffolding, given their skill struggles in this area. Figuring out how you'll start the conversation and what question you might ask in the first step, coupled with a reminder of the four tools used to gather information (questions, guesses, reflective listening, reassurance) will provide enough assistance to help get the first step off the ground. That said, there is only so much prep you can do for the first step of Plan B. It is always an adventure, and you want to be open-minded and prepared for surprises.

You will find that, if you do Plan B well, students will come to you and be willing to share more than they ever did, which means you may hear things you weren't prepared for. Ironically, the most important thing to do, when hit with a surprise with very serious implications, is not to take action but rather to gather information. What is the best way to gather information in those situations? Hold on tightly to your four tools from the first step of Plan B. Reflect what you heard, provide reassurance, ask questions, and if need be, take guesses. If you are ever feeling stuck or really thrown for a loop, you cannot go wrong with reflective listening and reassurance before asking some more questions to clarify things.

The second step of Plan B is perhaps the most important one to prepare in advance. If you are preparing to have a proactive problem-solving conversation, there is no reason to have to figure out your concerns and how to express them while on the fly. Rather, you have the luxury of clarifying your concerns, and even deciding exactly how you will communicate them to the student, ahead of time. This is where you and the team will ask yourselves: Why are you worried about this problem? Why are you wanting to have a conversation with the student in the first place? Remember the four categories of adult concerns from Chapter 6: health, safety, learning, and impact on others. And remember that the goal is to be as specific as possible when articulating your concerns. All kinds of interesting things can happen when a team is asked to articulate their concerns about a particular problem. Sometimes the team is unable to articulate a concern, which may lead them to decide that they should be using Plan C. At other times, you may find out that different team members have different concerns, and you may need to decide which are most important to pursue first. Whoever will be doing Plan B will be trying to best represent the entire team's concerns, so a discussion about them ahead of time is helpful. Just as you did with the opening observation, you should write down exactly how you will communicate your concerns to the student when it comes time.

Having done this preparation, you know how you will start Plan B, you've got some ideas about how to facilitate information gathering using the four tools, and you have your concerns ready to share with the student once you've identified the student's concerns. Then the only thing left completely to chance is the third step, where you will be brainstorming solutions together. Of course, you can't prepare for this step until you've identified the student's concerns. Remember, however, that you do have some handy scripts to use to kick off the brainstorming, which we shared in Chapter 6.

We have developed what we call the Plan B Prep Sheet to help structure the process described above (see Appendix B). You will notice that it guides you through all of the questions you need to answer when preparing for a Plan B conversation. Again, the ultimate goal is to not always need a Prep Sheet, but especially in the beginning, it can be helpful. If a student asks about the Prep Sheet, remember that one of the benefits of the Plan B process is that there is no secret that you need to hold back from the student. In fact, you can have them look over the Prep Sheet with you and plan for the conversation that is coming. Tell the student you are going to work hard to understand her point of view about the problem before you ask her to consider yours, and finally you will work together toward a solution. You can even explain that the reason you are using the Plan B Prep Sheet is that we adults have a hard time sticking to this kind of process instead of telling a student how we think a problem should be solved. You can explain that you are using the Prep Sheet to help you make sure you are solving the problem in a way that works for them, too.

## ACCOMMODATING SKILL STRUGGLES DURING PLAN B

Part of all good skills training is, of course, meeting the student at his current skill level and then building skills from there. As such, you will want to pay close attention to where each student gets stuck in the Plan B process. That information will serve as a clue about where you may need to build in some accommodations to help scaffold the skill building. Let's take a look at what some such accommodations look like in Plan B.

If you believe that the student has skill struggles in the area of language and communication, or you notice during problem solving that a student has hard time letting you know what her concerns are, you should feel free to do more educated guessing, or even to give her sentence starters like those in Box 9.1. Also remember that not all communication of concerns needs to be verbal. Be creative with forms of nonverbal communication, like journaling, drawing, signs, storyboards, the use of play and games, and even assistive technology.

| **BOX 9.1. OFFER SENTENCE STARTERS TO STUDENTS WHO HAVE TROUBLE LISTING CONCERNS.** |
| --- |
| It bothers me when . . . |
| I have a hard time with . . . |
| I don't like when . . . |
| I'm worried that . . . |
| It's hard for me because I need to . . . |
| It's hard for me because I want to . . . |

If you suspect attention and working memory skill deficits, or notice that a student struggles with focusing his attention or holding the information in mind necessary to do Plan B (such as remembering what his and your concerns are), you will want to provide some support in those areas. Fidget toys or some motoric activity or outlet can be helpful to facilitate focus, and you might want to suggest a way to assist his memory, such as a whiteboard for taking notes or a trifold board to represent the three steps of Plan B.

If you have noted that a student struggles with emotion- and/or self-regulation skills or observe frequent dysregulation during Plan B conversations, some sensorimotor activity before or during Plan B can be helpful. In some cases, your school's occupational therapist may have good ideas for you. In other cases, something as simple as a rhythmic, repetitive activity like playing catch, the game of Uno, or listening to music together can help. For those students whose emotional dysregulation is quickly triggered, you can also accommodate by starting with easier problems, leaning heavily on your regulating tools (reassurance and reflection), and being prepared to race back to the first step if the student escalates when you raise your concern.

If it is cognitive flexibility skills that appear to be the greatest challenge for a particular student, you will want to make sure the student is forewarned that you will want to talk about this problem (with plenty of reassurance), rather than catching her off guard in the hallway. Perhaps most importantly, you can help scaffold the process by preteaching the student the steps of Plan B. That way she will know exactly what to expect from the process so it can be predictable to her. You may find it helpful to write out the steps of Plan B for the student clearly and in order, checking each off as you go. You may even want to make a list of advantages and disadvantages for each suggested solution, to help a less flexible student move off of an original idea.

Finally, if you have hypothesized about deficits in the area of social thinking skills, the student may struggle with several different aspects of Plan B. You can help meet this student at his level by using clear verbal explanations of nonverbal behaviors (either those that have contributed to the problem, or those occurring during the conversation itself) and explicitly describing the student's impact on others in a way that may not be necessary for students without lagging social thinking skills. Of course, you will need to couple both of these things with lots of empathy and a reminder that you know he is doing the best he can in order to keep the student regulated and make sure he does not feel blamed.

In a small number of cases, you may find that a particular student could benefit from some additional, more didactic skills training. For instance, a student struggling with social thinking skills may actually benefit from being taught how to read certain nonverbal cues, or a student struggling with emotion-regulation skills may benefit from learning some relaxation strategies. In these cases, you might choose to augment frequent problem-solving conversations with more targeted skills training. We tackle this topic in Chapter 10, but it is worth noting that we find this to be true a minority of the time. Most of the time, students' skills can be built merely through repetition of the relational process of Plan B. As we discussed earlier, one of the great advantages of Plan B is that the skills training is baked right in.

## TROUBLESHOOTING

Preparing as thoroughly as possible for Plan B can certainly maximize your chances for success. But, as we have explained previously, don't always expect Plan B to go smoothly, even when you are well prepared. Remind yourself that if problem solving with a student were easy, you probably would not need to be doing Plan B with that student in the first place. If the student struggles with problem-solving skills, we should not be surprised when problem solving with him is hard! Also remember how the hard work of Plan B is where new learning happens, the brain changes, and skills are built, and so we should welcome the hard work.

Despite the value of the hard work, understanding why Plan B goes awry is crucial for understanding how to address those challenges. When Plan B goes really well, it is typically because the educator is doing it well (what we call high-fidelity Plan B) over a fairly easy Problem with a student who trusts the educator and the process, and who has sufficient problem-solving skills. When Plan B is harder, it is typically because the educator is new to Plan B and hasn't yet learned how to do it well (low-fidelity Plan B), might be working on a really tough Problem with a student who doesn't trust her or the process yet, and/or who lacks some problem-solving skills. Any one of these factors can make Plan B tougher, and several of them together of course can make for the most challenging Plan B. Let's consider these factors one at a time and what to do about them.

## Fidelity to the Plan B Process

First, let's talk about *fidelity*, which is also sometimes called *integrity*. These are terms used to refer to the degree to which someone delivers a particular approach the way it was intended. There are many types of low-fidelity Plan B, and problems with fidelity can occur in any of the three steps. Perhaps you started Plan B by focusing on the challenging behavior instead of the problem situation, or you brought the problem up in such a way that the student feels blamed. In these cases, Plan B may be doomed from the outset. If the opening of Plan B was good, there are still many possible pitfalls during the first step. Most frequent is one we call *drive-by empathy*, which is when you begin to hear the student's perspective, but then move on too quickly. Classically, this sounds like: "I understand that you think the work is boring, but . . ." and then moving directly to the adult concern or solution. Drive-by empathy does not include enough use of the four tools to gather the specifics of the student's concern or perspective. There is particular risk of this occurring with a student who struggles with the skills necessary to identify and express her concerns. The opposite of drive-by empathy is *interrogating*. In these cases, the student has already expressed his concern, but you might try to hammer away even though there is no more information to give.

In the second step of Plan B, a common fidelity mistake occurs when we adults suggest a solution instead of naming a concern, which greatly restricts the process. For example, you might say, "My concern is that you have to sit still on the rug." That is actually not a concern; that is a solution at which you might arrive in order to address some other concerns, presumably those having to do with paying attention or distracting others. An example with older students might be: "My concern is that you have to hand in your homework." Believe it or not, homework itself is a solution to some concerns, such as practicing new material and demonstrating the capacity to master material independently. Additionally, as you learned in Chapter 6, the more specific the concern, the better the process goes.

In the third step, the most common fidelity error occurs when an adult forgets to give the student the first chance to generate a solution. Another common slip is to get all the way to the third step with two sets of concerns, then let the student's concern fall right back off the balance. For example, you might say, "I wonder what we can do so that you aren't distracting other students and are getting your work done?" Noticeably absent from that invitation to brainstorm are the student's concerns, which might be, for example, difficulty sitting still or needing help with assignments. We even find that sometimes adults revert back to solving the challenging behavior instead of the problem situation in the third step of Plan B. For instance, "I wonder how you can handle that without hitting next time around." Being mindful of fidelity in the third step means remembering that there must be two sets of concerns—not solutions—on the balance, and that you are trying to solve the Problem (the antecedent or situation), as opposed to the challenging behavior.

So how do you catch fidelity mistakes like these, and what do you do about them? As we mentioned earlier, doing Plan B in pairs is a great antidote to low fidelity in Plan B. Typically, it is much easier for someone else to catch where Plan B may be going awry. Additionally, we have found that one of the most powerful tools to monitor fidelity is recording your Plan B conversations. Simply listening to, or watching, your Plan B attempts again while you have one eye on the steps of Plan B often allows you to identify your own errors, and work to correct them. Additionally, we have a number of fidelity tools that can be used for rating yourself or your supervisees. These will be discussed further in Chapter 12. Just keep in mind that you shouldn't be too hard on yourself! There is no such thing as Plan B perfection. However, practice makes better for sure.

## Tough Problems

Even if you are doing high-fidelity Plan B, the process could be tough simply because you've chosen a really hard Problem to solve. What's the answer to this? First, start with lower-hanging fruit by picking an easier problem, or one that the student is particularly invested in solving. However, eventually you'll still need to confront bigger, tougher problems. When that time comes, keep in mind that big problems are often many nested smaller problems. Try breaking the problem down into its components and handle them one at a time. Practically, this may mean that instead of solving *recess*, you are solving the problem of transitioning out to recess, the problem of losing at recess games, the problem of coming in from recess, and the problem of transitioning back to work. Also, be sure you have the right people at the table to solve a particular problem. Perhaps there are others who are closer to the problem, who have more creative solutions, or are in positions from which they can enact solutions that others can't.

## Trust

Even if you are doing high-fidelity Plan B over a fairly easy Problem, it could not be going well because the student doesn't trust you or the process yet. This is of course particularly true with most behaviorally challenging students who have been on the receiving end of punitive school discipline. They have every reason to believe that Plan B will actually turn out to be thinly-veiled Plan A. For this reason, before you get started, you may want to explain the philosophy of the approach, as well as what the Plan B process will look like. In these cases, starting with an easier problem is also a good idea. Since a lack of trust often translates into a dysregulated student, you will want to make ample use of your regulating tools: reassurance and reflective listening. If the trust issue seems particularly acute, you can also do Plan B about doing Plan B! In other words, make the focus of your next Plan B conversation the fact that the student in question seems to have concerns about problem solving with you, and you imagine there is a good reason for that.

Another important consideration is bringing in someone whom the student does trust. That may be another person in the building, or someone at home. Sometimes the simple presence of a trusted individual can help a student stay better regulated, leading to Plan B going more smoothly. Finally, while this might seem like it goes without saying, it is important to engage in other forms of relationship building with students. As wonderful as we think Plan B is, if it is the only currency of your relationship, the whole relationship will be defined by problems, which may feel shaming to the student. Simple things like playing with the student or talking about her interests can go a long way toward building the relationship. Finally, keep in mind that the process of Plan B itself will ultimately help build trust, as long as you don't revert to Plan A when Plan B gets stuck.

### Skill Struggles

Even if you are doing Plan B with high fidelity, over a solvable problem, with a student who trusts you, it can still not be going well due to the student's (or your!) skill struggles (remember, we all have them!). In those instances, pay attention to where Plan B gets stuck, because Plan B can be one of your most powerful assessment tools. Knowing exactly where the problem-solving process gets stuck can confirm or disconfirm your hypotheses about the primary skills deficits that you listed on the student's CPS-APT, and can help you know how to better accommodate those skill struggles during problem solving, as we discussed earlier in this chapter. And, as outlined in Chapter 7, most of the skills on the CPS-APT are modeled and practiced merely by repeating the Plan B process. In the relatively few cases where a student's skills don't seem to be improving with repetitions of Plan B, you will want to turn to what we call collaborative skills training. That is the topic of the next chapter.

# CHAPTER 10
## WHEN STUDENTS ARE STUCK: DIRECT SKILLS TRAINING

*Every time Mr. Remy gets to the third step of Plan B with Tina, and invites her to come up with a solution, she says the same thing: "I don't know." Each time, Mr. Remy then models the brainstorming process for her, but he thinks she should be able to follow his example by now. While they have been solving a lot of problems, it is usually because of Mr. Remy's solutions. "What will happen when Tina encounters a problem and I'm not around?" he wonders. Mr. Remy feels that Tina may need more than just Plan B to help her build this skill.*

In Chapter 7, we described how the relational process of using Plan B naturalistically and effectively trains many of the neurocognitive skills found on the CPS-APT. In addition, the process of solving problems together clarifies which skills might not be coming along through the process of problem solving, and might require more explicit skills training. The process of problem solving using Plan B also builds the type of helping relationship you will need with your student to be able to take on training these skills more didactically, that is, with direct instruction.

So, when should you use didactic skills training? In two instances: When specific skill struggles continue to get in the way of solving problems using Plan B, or when you find you are relying heavily on your skills to solve problems during Plan B, and the student's skills do not seem to be developing just through the process of modeling and practicing alone. Before we go into the details of what didactic skills training looks like using Plan B, it is important to note that while most educators gravitate naturally to more didactic forms of skills training, didactic skills training is actually far tougher than training skills through the naturalistic process of Plan B, for two reasons: First, didactic skills instruction requires students to admit that they have skill struggles and that they are open to you helping them practice and develop those skills. Second, didactic skills training requires transfer of these skills from the practice environment to the real world. You'll recall from Chapter 7 that these challenges of didactic skills training are two of the many reasons we prefer naturalistic skills training through problem solving, in which the student doesn't even need to know that he is practicing skills, and transfer of the skills isn't an issue. Due to these challenges of conducting didactic skills training successfully, we recommend that it be done the minority of the time, and only after you have done a lot of problem solving through Plan B. Remember, by solving lots of problems together with Plan B, you will establish a helping relationship, and a better awareness of the types of problems that are still a challenge for this particular student.

We refer to didactic skills training in CPS as *collaborative skills training*. The collaborative nature is crucial. If it's not done collaboratively, the student can feel as if the skills training is being done *to* them, rather than *with* them, thereby increasing the power differential between you and the student, and simultaneously increasing the chances that the student just goes through the motions without really learning. How many times have you had conversations with a student about practicing skills, and it sounds like they are just telling you exactly what they think you want to hear to get the conversation over with as quickly as possible? In collaborative skills training, the student should be coauthor of the skills-training process. The way to do this is to rely on the three steps of Plan B as your framework. Using those same three steps during didactic skills training that you learned in collaborative problem solving will ensure that the skills-training process is still collaborative, relational, and reciprocal. In doing this, you correct for many of the limitations of standard didactic skills training. So, what's the difference then between collaborative *skills training* and collaborative *problem solving*? The difference is simply the focus. In collaborative skills training, the focus shifts from the *Problem* to the *skills* that will be trained.

The first step of collaborative skills training still involves clarifying your student's perspective, but this time you will want to get her perspective about the skill to be built, as opposed to her perspective about the problem. You start this type of Plan B conversation the same way, with an empathic and neutral observation, but about the skill struggle rather than the trigger or expectation that has been difficult. You will also still rely upon the same four tools that you already learned in Chapter 6 to gather information (reflective listening, reassurance, educated guessing, and clarifying questions). You can even use the same sentence starters for your neutral observation. An example would be: "I've noticed that sometimes it seems hard during problem solving for you to come up with ideas for solutions to the problem. Have you noticed that?" It is critical that you then stop and gather information about the student's perspective. If the student does not agree that this skill is hard for her, resist the temptation to try to convince her that she lacks the skill; rather, listen hard. If she takes offense at the suggestion, remember your regulating tools (reflective listening and reassurance). In our experience, when the skill struggle is introduced through an empathic and neutral observation like this, many students will not only be able to accept your observation without feeling criticized, but also sometimes chuckle at the observation because it has become so blatantly obvious by virtue of your earlier problem-solving efforts.

If, after gathering information, you find that the student recognizes the skill struggle, you can proceed to the second step of Plan B, where you share your adult concern. But again, in collaborative skills training, you will be sharing your concern about the skill, as opposed to the problem situation. This step is often much easier in collaborative skills training, since the student will often share your concern about the impact of the skill struggle. If at that point you have both perspectives about the skill struggle under consideration, and a regulated student in front of you, it is safe to proceed to the final step of Plan B, where the collaboration begins. Here, you will be inviting the student to brainstorm not solutions to a problem, but rather ways to practice the skill together. Unlike problem solving with Plan B, in which you are attempting to reconcile two sets of concerns, in collaborative skills training—if the student agrees about the skill struggle—you are simply trying to jointly develop a plan to practice the skill you are both concerned about. If at any point the student shows reluctance to participate, you will go right back to the first step to re-regulate her and gather information about why she might be resistant.

Collaborative skills training can be used to initiate practice of virtually any skill. We find that there are some frequent culprits, however, which lend themselves better to collaborative skills training and/or are often stubborn skills that can require a little extra focus. Let us give a few examples of skills that we find ourselves most often training collaboratively. The first skill we will discuss is a student's ability to express his concerns. If a student has only mild skill struggles in the language and communication domain, regular Plan B ought to get the job done, with some additional scaffolding by using more educated guessing than you would otherwise. However, with more significant lagging language skills, you might need to do some didactic skills training using Plan B, such as in the example below.

> MRS. MORROW: We've noticed that you've been asking to take a lot of breaks lately, but it seems hard for you to tell us why you need a break when we ask. Have you noticed that, too?
>
> OLIVER: I don't know.
>
> MRS. MORROW: It's okay, you're not in trouble *(reassurance)*. I know you're trying your best, and I'm just trying to understand. I've noticed there are other times when it's hard for you to let us know what is bothering you, too. Do you think this is just something that's tough for you *(educated guess)*?
>
> OLIVER: I guess. I mean, sort of.
>
> MRS. MORROW: Okay, so it seems sort of hard for you. I wonder . . . Is it that you know what's bothering you and it's hard for you to find the words for it? Or you don't even know what's bothering you *(clarifying question)*?

**OLIVER:** If I know, I can tell you.

**MRS. MORROW:** So if you're aware of what's bothering you, you can tell us, but the times you don't tell us it's because you don't know what it is *(reflective listening)*?

**OLIVER:** Yeah.

**MRS. MORROW:** Okay, that's really helpful to know. *(Moves to second step.)* And I guess what I'm worried about is that if we don't know what's bothering you, it's really hard for us to help. *(Moves to third step.)* I bet there is a way for us to work together on figuring out what's bothering you and how to tell it to us so that we are better able to help you. Would you be up for that?

**OLIVER:** Sure.

**MRS. MORROW:** Okay, do you have any ideas about how we could practice that together?

Notice how Mrs. Morrow used all four tools in the first step to gather some really critical information. She also relied on the scripts in the second and third steps to frame the discussion. And instead of starting brainstorming by stating two competing concerns, she simply asked for ideas of how to jointly practice the skill (identifying what's bothering Oliver) in a way that helps her address her concern about the impact of that skills deficit. Finally, notice how she also gives Oliver the first opportunity to come up with a plan.

We are often surprised at the creative methods students generate to practice certain skills. But there are also plenty of times when they will draw a blank. With collaborative skills training, don't expect your students to necessarily have great ideas about how to practice skills. You should be ready to jump in with good ideas you have, but only after giving them first try at it and then asking if they would mind if you suggested something. When you do suggest a potential idea, pose it tentatively, asking the student what he thinks of your idea, and be willing to abandon it if the student isn't on board. Because direct skill instruction is the more prevalent form of skills training in schools, there are no shortage of curricula to serve as guides. You can bring those ideas to the table when doing collaborative skills training, but make sure the student agrees that they are good ideas. Let's get back to the example.

> **MRS. MORROW:** Would you mind if I suggested some ways we might practice this skill together?
>
> **OLIVER:** Okay.
>
> **MRS. MORROW:** I wonder if we could take some guesses together about all the different reasons you might need a break, and write them down somewhere, so when you need a break, we can check the list together. What do you think?
>
> **OLIVER:** I guess. But how would we always have the list with us?
>
> **MRS. MORROW:** I don't know. I guess it would have to be a list that we could have with us most of the time. Any ideas about how we might do that?
>
> **OLIVER:** Maybe we could put it on flashcards or something?
>
> **MRS. MORROW:** Sure! So let's see if we can come up with a list of all the different reasons you could need a break, and write them on flashcards that you can keep in your binder.

You'll notice in this example that the student has decent enough language and communication skills to participate in this collaborative skills training discussion. A student with more severe communication skills deficits might need the team to develop the list of possible reasons for needing a break in advance of the discussion, and merely run them by the student to see if they make sense and seem appropriate. If a student has no communication, the team may need to develop the list and a plan for how to experiment with it without the student's involvement. In other words, collaborative skills training should always be as collaborative as possible, but sometimes, given a student's skill level, it may need to be less collaborative than is ideal. Remember that the concept of scaffolding that we discussed earlier: You want to do just enough of the work to move the process forward, but not too much, so the student gets practice. In this example, Mrs. Morrow and

Oliver end up creating a small deck of flashcards with these expressions on them:

- My brain has been working hard.
- My body has been working hard.
- I want to talk or problem solve with an adult.
- I'm ready for some quiet time.
- I'm not sure.
- There's another reason.

When Oliver said he needed the break, but couldn't say why, they would quickly flip through the cards together, and Oliver would select the one that was most accurate. Over a period of only a few months, they stopped needing the cards because they both knew the list. By the end of the year, all Mrs. Morrow needed to do was ask why Oliver needed a break, and he was able to verbalize one of those options. Even more exciting was the fact that, when Oliver switched schools the next year, the skill stayed firmly in place.

Let's move on to our second category of skill struggles, which is attention and working memory skills. One of the most common situations in which we utilize collaborative skills training is when a student has difficulty generating and weighing possible solutions to a problem. (Note that this task, in addition to working memory, also may involve cognitive flexibility, so it will be important to work with the student to understand which part of the task is hard.) This is a great example of how problem solving using Plan B can clarify the skill struggles that are not coming along through the naturalistic and relational process of training skills. Remember Mr. Remy's struggles with Tina at the beginning of this chapter? Students like Tina draw a blank every time you get to the third step of Plan B and ask them to generate a solution. Even after giving ample time to think, they may say, "I don't know." You will find yourself doing a lot of brainstorming aloud for the student in this case, which can lead to successful solutions, but the skill may not get trained. Having had that shared experience, you are in a great position to name the skill struggle and facilitate collaborative skills training. If Mr. Remy were to try collaborative skills training, it might look like this:

> MR. REMY: You know what I've noticed? When we're doing problem solving together, and it gets to the part when I ask you whether you have any ideas for solutions . . .
>
> TINA: I never have any?
>
> MR. REMY *(chuckles)*: Well, maybe not never. But it seems hard for you to come up with ideas. So you have noticed that too, huh?
>
> TINA: Yeah, my mind just goes blank.
>
> MR. REMY: So are you saying it's not that you have ideas that you think aren't good, you actually don't have any at all *(clarifying question)*?
>
> TINA: Exactly.
>
> MR. REMY: So your mind goes blank and you don't have ideas. *(Moves to the second step.)* And I guess I'm worried that if you have a lot of trouble with that, and there's nobody to help you come up with ideas, you might get stuck when you're trying to solve problems on your own. *(Moves to the third step.)* So, I wonder if there is some way to practice what to do when your mind goes blank so you'll be in better shape when there's nobody there to help.

In this particular instance of collaborative skills training, you are going to want to be ready with some potential ideas for how to work on coming up with solutions. Otherwise, you'll be in the ironic position of asking a student who has a hard time coming up with ideas to come up with ideas for how to come up with ideas! It is always worth giving the student a chance, but there is a framework for you to rely on if indeed her mind draws a blank (Greene, 2005; Greene & Ablon, 2005).

> MR. REMY: So I know this is sort of funny to ask, but do you have any ideas for how we could practice that?
>
> TINA *(smiling)*: I don't know.
>
> MR. REMY: Well, I guess this is a good example. Would you mind if I suggested a way to practice?

TINA: Sure.

MR. REMY: I was taught that there are really only three different types of solutions. The first is meeting in the middle, also known as compromising. The second is asking someone to lend a hand, which you can always do. And the third is doing something another way than you've done before. A good way to remember the three options is the acronym MAD: Meet in the middle, ask for a hand, do it another way. And I don't know about you, but if I can't come up with a solution to a problem, that's how I feel: Mad! Does that make sense?

*— Meet in middle*
*— Ask for a hand*
*— Do it another way.*

TINA: I think so, sort of.

MR. REMY: Let me give you a couple examples. If you and one of your classmates were in the lunch line and you both reached for the last chocolate milk at the same time, you could say to yourself: What would meeting in the middle look like?

TINA: Split it?

MR. REMY: Yes! And how about asking for a hand?

TINA: Well, I guess we could ask if there were any more chocolate milks.

MR. REMY: Good! And what would doing it another way look like?

TINA: I guess maybe one of us would have to get something different to drink?

MR. REMY: Exactly. So there, you just came up with three different solutions. Depending on what the problem is, some options will work better than others. So what do you think, can we practice reminding ourselves of those three options to see if they give us some ideas?

TINA: Sure.

What we have observed with many students like Tina over time is that in the beginning they need to be reminded of the acronym MAD, but before long they remember the three options themselves, and eventually don't even need to be prompted because the template to generating solutions has been laid. A reminder: As we discussed in Chapter 8, when you're trying to build a new skill, you are trying to create a new pathway in the brain. The path that currently goes straight to "I don't know" for Tina will eventually go to MAD. But this requires repetition with small doses of good stress (meaning it won't be easy for Tina at first) embedded within the context of this relational interaction. Also note that practicing generating solutions over a hypothetical issue like the chocolate

---

**M**EET IN THE MIDDLE

**A**SK FOR A HAND

**D**O IT ANOTHER WAY

---

milk in this example is unlikely to generalize to the real problems Tina is having a hard time solving. For this reason (remember the specificity principle of neuroplasticity), it is critical that this practice occurs over real problems in real time. This initial collaborative skills training discussion has simply put a plan in place for the next time problem solving gets stuck in the third step of Plan B over a chronic problem that has been occurring for the student. At that time, Mr. Remy and Tina can practice using MAD in the context of a real problem, and that's where the best learning happens!

The next category of skill struggles to discuss is emotion- and self-regulation skills. Easily dysregulated students are often the students who exhibit the most frequent challenging behaviors in the face of difficulties, and they are also most likely to have trouble even tolerating problem-solving conversations with an adult. The good news is that students who have trouble managing frustration, disappointment, anger, sadness, and worry will build their ability to do so through your repeated, calm modeling of the Plan B steps when solving problems together. This gentle delivery of stress at just the level that is manageable for a student is called *exposure*, and exposure will slowly stretch a student's ability to manage more and more negative emotion.

* see p. 174

For a student who seems to need a little more practice staying regulated than what solving problems using Plan B provides, you may want to look for other opportunities for exposure. Since we know that gradual exposure to a dysregulating emotion or experience is the key to being able to eventually tolerate that emotion or experience, finding a balance of just enough exposure to stress the system without overwhelming it is critical. As such, it is especially important to get the student's perspective of how to find that balance. This is where Plan B comes into play with collaborative skills training for emotion-regulation skills. Let's look at an example.

In the following vignette, the teacher hasn't been able to get very far in Plan B conversations with Charisse because Charisse, who tends to be very nervous in many social situations, avoids conversations with her.

**MRS. NORMAN:** It seems like when I ask you to problem solve with me, you find something else to do or rush through and say you have somewhere else to go. What's going on?

**CHARISSE:** I don't know.

**MRS. NORMAN:** Don't worry, I'm not upset with you. I can think of a few reasons you might not want to have these conversations *(reassurance)*. I guess I'm wondering if it makes you feel nervous or anxious to talk to me about the things that are hard for you *(educated guess)*.

**CHARISSE:** Yeah, I guess. I don't like talking about it. It's awkward.

**MRS. NORMAN:** It feels awkward to talk to me in general? Or just about these sorts of things *(clarifying questions)*?

**CHARISSE:** It's fine when we're doing math or whatever. But whenever we have to talk about other stuff, serious stuff, it feels awkward, and yeah, I guess I get nervous that I'll say something dumb.

**MRS. NORMAN:** That makes sense *(reassurance)*. A lot of students feel nervous talking to adults, especially about important or serious things. *(Moves to second step.)* My concern is that I want you to be able to get help when you need it, and learning to talk to adults and others about important stuff will make it more likely that you'll always get the help you need. *(Moves to third step.)* I wonder if there are things we can do that will help you manage feeling nervous when you talk to adults so that you'll be able to get the help you need. Can you think of anything?

CHARISSE: I'd rather just not have to talk.

MRS. NORMAN: Well, sure, that's one idea, and not talking may help you not feel nervous, but will it help you build the skill of talking to other people when you need help?

CHARISSE: I guess not.

MRS. NORMAN: If there was a way to practice talking with adults without feeling too nervous, would you try it?

CHARISSE: Without feeling nervous, sure! But how?

MRS. NORMAN: Well, I do have an idea, but I would only want to try it out if you were up for it.

CHARISSE: What's the idea?

MRS. NORMAN: Well, the best way to get over being nervous about something is to try little, tiny bits of it, then when you can do that much without being nervous, you try a little more, and then a little more. So for instance, if you can tell me something, besides math, that we can talk about that might make you feel a tiny bit nervous, but not as nervous as when we talk about the serious stuff, we can start there.

CHARISSE: Like if I talk about my field hockey team?

MRS. NORMAN: Yes, that's a great idea. Will talking about your field hockey team with me make you feel a little awkward, but not uncomfortably nervous?

CHARISSE: Yes, because it's sort of weird to talk to you about something other than math anyway!

MRS. NORMAN: Great, let's meet just to talk about that, for as many times as it takes. Once talking about field hockey doesn't make you feel nervous at all, we can talk about something maybe just a little more serious, and see how that goes. And you can tell me at any time if it gets to be too much, Okay?

CHARISSE: Okay.

Notice how, in this conversation with Charisse, the anxiety was around talking with adults, so Mrs. Norman was also the one delivering the exposure. This gets slightly more complicated when the student's anxiety is around something less under the teacher's control. For instance, one of the trickiest situations in which we are often called on to do collaborative skills training is when a student is exhibiting school refusal (more appropriately called school anxiety). When a student is anxious about attending school in the first place, it can be very hard to stick to the steps of Plan B (mostly because the adults start getting dysregulated too, given how much is riding on the conversation), but that is exactly what is needed if you are going to put together a plan to expose the student to attending school in doses he can handle. The risk of exposing too fast and overwhelming the student's ability to regulate himself is too great. So how do you know how much stress is enough to stretch the skills, but not enough to be overwhelming? The answer is more simple than you think: Ask the student! In the first step, use your four tools to find out as much as you can about what, specifically, causes the student anxiety. In the second step you can concisely share your concern for the student's learning. In the third step, just as with Charisse, you can briefly teach the student what we know about exposure, then invite the student to coauthor a plan for starting with the lowest level of exposure that won't feel overwhelming, and assure the student that you will be getting his feedback at every step, for when he is ready to increase the exposure and when it feels like too much. Remember that reassurance is a powerful regulating tool. In the case of school refusal, reassure the student that you will not force him to be exposed to more than he feels he can handle (which would be Plan A). In our experience, with patience and collaboration, and by not giving up on the approach when small setbacks happen, students can not only build emotion- and self-regulation skills through coauthored exposure, but they do so while building confidence in their ability to address problems that arise, and while building a helping relationship with the caring adults around them.

The next category of skills deficits is cognitive flexibility. Within the cognitive flexibility domain, many students struggle with the types of cognitive distortions we discussed in Chapter 4. Collaborative skills training can be used to help "gray up" the black-and-white thinking of students who suffer from cognitive distortions. This process has been referred to as *cognitive restructuring* by cognitive behavioral therapists. When this is the skill on which you are focusing, the goal of the first step of Plan B is to empathize with the bias or distortion in the student's thinking. Remember, to empathize, you don't have to agree with the distorted point of view or debunk it, you just need to understand it. The second step of Plan B includes sharing your idea about the distortions, which usually means suggesting a more nuanced perspective of the situation in question. Finally, in the third step, you are inviting the student to work together with you to discover what the most accurate perspective is: Is it their distorted view or your grayer interpretation that is closer to reality? Your job is to do what the father of cognitive therapy, Dr. Aaron Beck, called *collaborative empiricism*. You are inviting the student to be a researcher with you and answer the question of where the truth actually lies. Just remind yourself at the outset to be open-minded. If the data actually support the student's perspective, maybe it was not a distortion after all! We cannot ask our students to be open to a different interpretation if we ourselves are not as well. Let's take the common example of a student whose distortion is: "I'm stupid, I can't do this!" Imagine that in this particular student's case that you completed a CPS-APT, which confirmed that this distortion and the related disparaging statement occurs most often in the context of challenging math.

> **MR. PEETE:** So I've noticed that when we're working on math, you will often say that you're stupid and you can't do the work. Have you noticed that?
>
> **JAMISON:** Well yeah, because it's true. *(Note that almost any adult will respond to this by kindly pointing out that the student is not stupid. This would actually be a misstep in Plan B. Convincing the student that he is wrong is not empathy. Stick with the script!)*

**MR. PEETE:** So you say that you're stupid because you think it's true *(reflective listening)*.

**JAMISON:** I *know* it's true. If I wasn't stupid, I'd be able to do it.

**MR. PEETE:** So because you have a hard time with math sometimes, you feel like you're stupid *(reflective listening)*. *(Moves to the second step by suggesting a grayer interpretation.)* I guess what I'm thinking is that you do have a hard time with math sometimes, but I'm not sure that makes you stupid.

**JAMISON:** Well, the smart kids don't have a problem with math!

**MR. PEETE:** *(Needs to regulate Jamison, so moves back to the first step.)* I hear what you're saying. You see some kids not having a hard time with math, and you think those are the smart kids. So if you're having a hard time with math, you must not be smart. *(Note that Mr. Peete is not agreeing, just reflecting. But having re-regulated the student, he goes back to the second step again, suggesting a grayer interpretation.)* I guess I assume everyone in the class is working on something, and you are working on math, but there are other things you are great at.

**JAMISON:** No, there aren't.

**MR. PEETE:** *(Moves back to the first step again.)* So it feels like there's nothing you're good at in school *(reflective listening)*. Well, if you can't think of anything you're good at, I can see why you say you feel stupid then! *(Tries the second step again.)* And I guess I feel like I see lots of examples of where you do things well, even though you have a hard time with math. *(Goes for the third step.)* I bet there is something we can do to figure out together whether you are really not good at most things at school, or whether you have a hard time at math but do well at lots of other things. Can you think of a way we can figure that out together?

**JAMISON:** We don't need to because I already know.

**MR. PEETE:** *(Moves back to the first step of Plan B to re-regulate Jamison.)* I hear you. You feel like it's not even worth checking this out because you're pretty sure you're not one of the smart kids *(reflective listening)*. *(Tries second step, with gray, tentative language.)*

And maybe I'm wrong, but it could be that perhaps there are lots of things you are good at. So I think it may be worth doing an experiment together just to see. How would we do that?

JAMISON: You could count up all the times I do something stupid. Then you'll see.

MR. PEETE *(following the script)*: That's one idea! And I guess if we counted all those up, we would have to also count all the times you didn't struggle, and even the times you were doing great. I wonder if we could do that together?

JAMISON: I guess, but I don't know how we would do it anyway.

MR. PEETE: Well, like I started out saying, I've noticed that you've been saying you're stupid during math, so I think it would be easy to count up the times you're struggling with math. Maybe I could also pay attention to times when you're not struggling, and ask, if that's true, whether we should put it on the list of things you're good or great at.

Cognitive restructuring like this requires looking for disconfirming evidence when it exists, so as to come to a more accurate interpretation of information. In this case, Mr. Peete and Jamison created a list together with three columns: things at which Jamison was great, things at which Jamison was good, and things with which Jamison struggled. Lo and behold, he did struggle at math, but there were many items each day in the other two columns. When looking at the data together, they agreed that perhaps "I'm stupid" wasn't accurate, and that, "I'm having trouble with math, but I'm good at a lot of other things" was more accurate. Not only did they correct a cognitive distortion, but also a student who has the latter explanation in mind during math will have an easier time dealing with those struggles than a student who interprets problems in math as an indicator that he is sorely lacking across the board. No matter the content of the specific distortion, you can use this same process to collaborate with your students to find the most realistic interpretation of situations. Notably, by following the steps of Plan B, this cognitive restructuring process occurs within a relational interaction that also validates the student's self worth.

The final category of skill struggles is our social thinking skills category. Many educators have been trained to help students practice social skills. There is an abundance of good curricula to provide great ideas for how to practice all kinds of social thinking skills. By all means, you should use those to your advantage. However, as we discussed at the outset of this chapter, it is absolutely critical that skills training be as collaborative as possible so as to maintain the relational context that is so crucial to changing the brain. So just as in our example where Mr. Remy used the acronym MAD, you can come prepared with ideas how you might help a student practice certain social thinking skills and start out with a hypothetical example, but be ready to apply the new skills in the real-life situations with which the student struggles. Also remember that if the skills training is done *to* the student without the student being coauthor of the process, there is much greater likelihood that the student will go through the motions without really being engaged in the process. So be open to the possibility that the student may have different or better ideas, or just simply not like yours. The last thing you want to do is impose a form of skills training on a student, i.e., use Plan A to try to build a skill. We have learned to trust the process of Plan B even when we don't know exactly where it is going to lead. You will be surprised at how your students come up with some fantastic ways to practice skills that you may never have thought of. In the following example, the teacher wants to help a student develop the skill of knowing where her body is in space and how to join a group, sometimes called *right of entry* skills.

> **MRS. CONCANNON:** Gabe, it seems like there are some times where you want to join in with a group of friends, and people end up getting a little frustrated with you. Have you noticed that?
>
> **GABE:** You mean like when I get too close to people?
>
> **MRS. CONCANNON:** You think you get too close to people?
>
> **GABE:** People say that I have to respect their personal space. They say I get too close and I annoy them.
>
> **MRS. CONCANNON:** Hm. People say you get too close to others, and they find that annoying (*reflective listening*). And what do you think of that?

GABE: I'm not sure it's true all the time.

MRS. CONCANNON: Okay, it's not true all the time, but you think sometimes it may be true?

GABE: I guess so, but I don't know. If I did, then I wouldn't be doing it!

MRS. CONCANNON: So it sounds like you have a hard time knowing if you're too close or not, and sometimes people get frustrated with you and that's confusing *(reflective listening)*. *(Moves to second step.)* And I guess what I'm worried about is that if you're not sure how to join your friends without getting too close to them, and if you're not even sure when you're doing it, it will be hard to fix the problem. Maybe you will end up even feeling like not trying.

GABE: Yeah, that's what I'm doing.

MRS. CONCANNON: And that stinks because you want to hang out with your friends. *(Moves to third step.)* So maybe we can think of a way to practice learning how to join your friends without getting too close, so you can hang out with your friends without upsetting them, and you won't feel so confused. *(Mrs. Concannon panics a little bit here, realizing she has no idea how to practice this. But she sticks with the script and invites Gabe to brainstorm solutions.)* Can you think of a way?

GABE: *(long pause)* I could measure the distance between my shoes and their shoes.

MRS. CONCANNON: *(Knowing that Gabe tends to be a bit concrete, Mrs. Concannon is a little worried that he is actually considering using a ruler, but she decides to get more information.)* That's an interesting idea. What do you mean?

GABE: Well, I could look down at the other kids and see how far apart their shoes are from each other, and I could put my shoes about the same distance from them.

MRS. CONCANNON: Wow, that's a good idea! I don't think I ever would have thought of that.

To most of us without this skill struggle, the process of walking up to a group and figuring out how close to stand is natural. For Gabe it is not. But through the collaborative skills training process of Plan B,

Gabe was able to generate a great idea for how to gather information and practice the skill in the naturalistic environment in which he was being asked to apply it. If Gabe did not have any ideas, Mrs. Concannon could feel free to suggest any she might be able to generate, including perhaps by using ideas from a social skills curriculum with which she is familiar. She would just need to remember to do so tentatively and collaboratively, and to make sure that Gabe agreed that it is a good way to practice the skill.

We've now given you an example of how to use the steps of Plan B to proceed with more direct skill instruction with a student struggling with skills in each of the five skill categories. Plan B provides a framework for introducing all kinds of methods to practice skills more didactically, while still ensuring that the process is collaborative, relational, and reciprocal with investment, ownership, and coauthorship from the student. Remember, this form of collaborative skills training is something we do the minority of the time, and only after a lot of problem solving, so we have established enough of a trusting relationship, and so that we have more information on which skills deficits might require this type of direct skills instruction.

# CHAPTER 11
## GROUP PLAN B: PROBLEM SOLVING WITH MULTIPLE STUDENTS

*Mrs. Stein approached her CPS trainer at the end of her first training day. "I work in a therapeutic school, and I don't just have problems with one or two students in my class," she said. "Sometimes it's the majority of the class not respecting a rule or triggering each other! How can I possibly have 10 different Plan B discussions with 10 different students, all over a single problem?"*

So far, we have only given examples of problem-solving conversations that are between one adult and one student. But there is another useful option that can be done with more than one student at a time, or even a whole class: Group Plan B. If you are having a problem with multiple students at the same time, and if you are sure that your expectations are clear and realistic, Group Plan B will be your best use of time. Remember that Plan B simply requires having a problem to solve in which there are competing perspectives, and in which a good solution will address all the perspectives. That could happen with one adult and one student, or with one adult and multiple students, or even one student and multiple adults. One of the most common uses of Group Plan B occurs when you are having a Plan B conversation with one student and it becomes clear that there is another person whose perspective needs to be heard. This is when individual Plan B quickly shifts to Group Plan B. Let's take a look at an example.

### SMALL GROUP PLAN B

In this example, Max had been frequently texting during class. On Wednesday, Max refused to put away his phone after being asked several times, and refused to relinquish his phone when the teacher tried to take it away. When the teacher then tried to escort him out of classroom, he escalated, shouting some rather creative obscenities. Because things were so tense between Max and the teacher following this most recent episode, Ms. Williams, the assistant principal, decided to initiate the Plan B conversation with Max.

MS. WILLIAMS: So it seems like it's been hard to resist using your phone in class. Can you fill me in?

MAX: (*Sits in silence.*)

MS. WILLIAMS: It sounds to me like you must have had a really important reason you didn't want to give up your phone (*reassurance*).

MAX: Well, it's mine, she can't just take my stuff.

MS. WILLIAMS: I hear you. Your phone does belongs to you, and you were upset that she tried to take it (*reflective listening*). I think the issue started around you texting in class, and it seems like it was really important to you to text (*reassurance*). Was something going on (*clarifying question*)?

MAX: Julian says I beat up my girlfriend, and it's all over the school.

MS. WILLIAMS (*steadying herself*): Wait, let me get this straight: Julian said you beat up Crystal?

MAX: Yes, and it's not true, but it's all over the school.

MS. WILLIAMS: Okay, we obviously need to talk about that, but what does this have to do with your phone?

MAX: I said it's all over school.

MS. WILLIAMS: Are you saying you were texting with people about it?

MAX: Yeah, I'm trying to stop the rumors and get Julian to shut up.

MS. WILLIAMS: I see. So you're monitoring the rumors and trying to stop it. Why would Julian say that?

MAX: I don't know, you'll have to ask him. But if I see him, I'm going to kick his ass.

**MS. WILLIAMS:** I can imagine how upset you are about this, if he's spreading really bad rumors that aren't true (*reassurance*). We need to get to the bottom of this. It sounds like I need to have a conversation with Julian also.

What happened with Ms. Williams and Max is something that happens often in Plan B. You start off thinking you have one problem to solve, and you end up in a very different place. Be prepared for surprises, and if you get thrown, you can't go wrong by gathering information. In this case, Ms. Williams did a good job of using her tools in the first step to gather information. It became clear that this problem was not about the phone. Max's phone use in class was a solution (albeit not a great one) to the actual problem, which was the fact of these very upsetting rumors. The next step was to find out Julian's perspective, and bring the two together into what we call Group Plan B. In a less emotionally charged situation, she may be able to bring Julian directly in. In a more charged situation like this one, it may be best to get a sense of Julian's perspective separately first. In this case, Ms. Williams talked with Julian and found out that he was unhappy with Max about his treatment of Crystal, and Julian agreed to join Max to talk about it together.

**MS. WILLIAMS:** Okay, Julian, thanks for talking to us. Nobody's in trouble, we're just trying to get to the bottom of what's been going on, and I want to hear from you. Max said that others have told him that you have been talking about him and Crystal. Can you tell me what's going on?

**JULIAN:** Ever since Max and Crystal have been going out, Crystal can't hang out with any of her old friends. I haven't been able to see her in weeks, and we used to be best friends!

**MAX:** So you told people I beat her up?

**JULIAN:** What? I didn't say you beat her! I said you were abusing her, by keeping her away from us.

**MAX:** Well, what's going around is that you said I beat her up. I never laid a hand on her!

**JULIAN:** I never said you did!

MS. WILLIAMS: Okay, I'm starting to understand. It sounds like part of this was an unfortunate misunderstanding, and Julian's words got twisted. But it also sounds like you two have an issue we need to work out. Julian, did I hear you right when you said that you and Crystal were best friends, and now you don't feel like you get to see her enough?

JULIAN: Enough? He doesn't let me see her at all! He doesn't let her hang out with any of her guy friends.

MAX: It has nothing to do with you being a guy. We've only been going out for a month, and I don't have much time to hang out with her either when I'm not at school or at work. So you and Crystal used to hang out after school together, but now that's the time we're together before I go to work.

MS. WILLIAMS: Let me see if I have this right. Julian, you used to hang out with Crystal after school, and you miss her. Now she's with Max after school. Max, you don't mind Crystal seeing Julian, but she's your girlfriend, and you have limited time to see her after school every day before you have to go to work. I wonder if there's any way that Julian can see Crystal more, and Max can spend all the time he wants with his girlfriend when he's not at school or work.

As with all the best Plan B conversations, once all perspectives are clarified and laid out, possible solutions that address all concerns become clear. As you might predict, Max and Julian decided that Julian would ask Crystal to hang out in the evenings, while Max was at work. Because both boys felt that they were being heard and their perspectives were taken into account in the solution, they were also calm enough to directly discuss the rumors. Julian admitted that it was a misunderstanding that led him to say that Max was "abusing" Crystal, and that he didn't intend for his words to be misconstrued and cause Max problems. He agreed to clarify the situation with the peers who had been spreading the rumors.

In this case, the teacher reported that once the problem giving rise to the texting was solved, Max's texting in class completely stopped.

The adult's concern was addressed without having to pursue it directly. In some cases, when you are facilitating Group Plan B between two or more students, you will still need to express the adult concern. The goal then is to find a solution that addresses everyone's concerns, including yours. Thankfully, however, most of our adult concerns related to conflict between students fall by the wayside once the conflict is resolved, as in the case with Max and Julian.

It is worth noting that other strategies exist for successfully resolving conflict between peers. For example, peer mediation is a powerful tool that has become more common, particularly in high school settings. Group Plan B can provide a perfect, easy-to-follow framework for facilitating peer mediation. Peer mediators are taught the steps of Plan B so that they can play the role of the assistant principal in the example with Max and Julian. With peer mediation, the mediating peer does not enter his or her concern into the mix, but rather clarifies the concerns of both parties and then invites them to work together to generate a solution that works for both of them. The peer mediator's job is to help ensure that a solution is found that does truly address each party's concerns, is realistic, and is practical. Having peers lead the process by definition reduces the power differential, and feels far less punitive. The challenge, of course, even for the most skilled peer, is navigating complex social interactions with heightened emotions. The steps of Plan B and the four tools of the first step in particular give the peer mediator a clear road map. In fact, mediators can even share the steps of this structured process with the peers whom they are attempting to help.

## LARGE GROUP PLAN B

Group Plan B can also be used with larger clusters of students and even an entire classroom. Many social-emotional curricula utilize community meetings, such as morning meeting from the Responsive Classroom and Open Circle. Plan B can provide a great structure for the process of these community meetings whenever there is a problem that impacts, involves, or influences a majority of students in the class. The goal of the process will be to get everyone's concerns and perspectives heard before adding your own (if that is even necessary), and then inviting the group to collaborate on potential solutions.

There are a few things to keep in mind before setting out to do this type of Group Plan B. As in any large group discussion, you'll want to set clear expectations for how the discussion will go. For younger students, you may want to put some structure in place so it is clear who is talking and who is listening; for instance, a talking stick or rock or ball that is passed to the person who is speaking. Other guidelines to be discussed involve encouraging others to share their point of view while avoiding you-statements that likely lead to blaming others in the class. Make it clear that you will invite everyone to share their perspective, but students do not have to do so if they don't feel comfortable. It is also helpful to preview with the whole group what the sequence of the three steps will look like. That way, you can remind the students to hold off on suggesting any potential solutions until all concerns are heard. This is a good opportunity to remind students that any idea is a good idea that you will test out together to see if it might make for a good solution. It is often helpful to have a student take the role of recording students' concerns as they are expressed. This can be done on a flip chart, whiteboard, or smartboard. In many cases, once all the concerns are written down, they can be combined or grouped to reduce the list to a manageable size. It is also important to consider that you may not get through all three steps of Group Plan B in one discussion, and you can give your students a heads up that this may be the case. Following is an example of large Group Plan B.

> **MRS. SCHULMAN:** So, friends, I've been noticing that it's been a little bit of a struggle lately for us to line up at the door calmly and quietly when it's time to go to specials. I was hoping that we could use our circle time this morning to talk about that. Let's remember how we take turns talking and listening. Has anyone else noticed that transitioning to specials has been hard? What do you think is going on? Why is it so hard?
>
> **JAMES:** Because it's so long to wait!
>
> **DUNCAN:** Yeah, and we have nothing to do but just stand there!

**MRS. SCHULMAN:** Okay. Fernanda, do you want to write down what your friends say so we can keep track? So far we have "long time to wait" and "nothing to do."

**WILL:** I don't like it because people are always pushing and shoving against me.

**MRS. SCHULMAN:** Ah, so people's bodies bump into each other? Anything else?

**ROBERTO:** I never get to go first in line.

**MRS. SCHULMAN:** So another issue is who gets to go first, and maybe that's why there is some pushing and shoving, too. Anything else that makes it hard? *(Waits out the silence.)* Okay, sounds like we have a lot of good reasons why it's hard. *(Moves to step two.)* And I guess I want to make sure that we get safely, quietly, and quickly from place to place, because I don't want us to miss learning time, distract other classes, or have friends getting hurt. *(Moves to step three.)* So what do you think we can do about this? Does anyone have ideas of how to solve this problem so it will work well for everybody?

**ROBERTO:** You could make sure everyone gets a turn to go first.

**DUNCAN:** You could give us something to do while we're waiting in line.

**ALEXA:** If we could line up quickly, we wouldn't need something to do.

**MRS. SCHULMAN:** Okay, those are good ideas. Remember, all ideas are good ideas. Let's write them all down.

**MARIANA:** What if we don't even get in a line while we wait?

**MRS. SCHULMAN:** What do you mean?

**MARIANA:** Well, if you're in a line, people are going to squoosh up against you. But we could be spread out while we're waiting so we're not so close to each other.

**JAMES:** But how would we know where to go?

**MARIANA** *(looks down at linoleum square tiles on the floor)*: We could each have our own square on the floor that we stand in.

**ROBERTO:** But how would we know who goes first?

**MARIANA:** We could each have a number, and we could change the first number every day.

**MRS. SCHULMAN:** Wow, these are some great ideas. What do you all think? Would this work for everyone?

**WILL:** Well, if we all knew which square to go to, and we stayed in our square, then we wouldn't push or shove people, and if we knew what order to go in, we could go quickly.

**ROBERTO:** But how would we pick who goes first!?

**MARIANA:** We could put all the names in a hat and pull them out in a different order every week.

The vignette above is based on a real example in which a student came up with a solution that probably never would have been suggested by a teacher. One of the most powerful moments of Plan B is when students come up with solutions after an adult has helped them clarify the perspectives. Most students almost reflexively turn to their teacher for solutions. We are always most impressed with the students when they are coauthors of the solution. Additionally, the students are usually more invested in these solutions too. In this case, students eagerly made small name cards that could be drawn out of a hat, and brainstormed ways to make it clear which linoleum square belonged to whom. When it came time to enact the solution, the students were very proud of how effective it was, and poured their energy into pulling it off.

## THE PROSOCIAL ENVIRONMENT

The success of Group Plan B rests not only on whether one adheres to the steps of the process, but also on the classroom and school culture itself. CPS can be a key ingredient of a prosocial classroom. Schools that have worked hard to create a prosocial environment find it easy to embrace the Group Plan B process because they have taught the students a number of key themes. These include:

- Everyone in the classroom has their own strengths and weaknesses.

- Everyone is working on something.
- Everyone can help someone else with something they are working on.

CPS extends these ideas, frequently applied to learning differences and social-emotional needs, to the behavioral realm. In our example of large Group Plan B, it is highly likely that the majority of students in the classroom had no trouble transitioning from homeroom to specials. In the absence of a prosocial environment, those students might object to spending time coming up with a solution to a problem that they feel they did not create. Similarly, they also might not be eager to have to try a different way of doing things when the original way worked just fine for them. In the prosocial classroom, those students realize that everybody, including themselves, is working on something, and it is their responsibility to help their peers with those things with which they struggle, just as their peers will be asked to do the same with them in some other circumstance. The frequent refrain from the prosocial teacher is: "Remember, everybody's working on something; in our class we help each other."

A teacher who is new to CPS, after working hard to arrive at solutions tailored to a particular student's concerns, might fear that there will be an uprising of other students who cry foul at what they perceive to be special treatment. But in any prosocial classroom, students learn that *fair does not mean equal*. Remind your students of the importance of doing different things for different people, ensuring that everyone gets what they need. When invariably one of your students shouts out: "That's not fair! How come she gets to use the fidget toy, and I don't?" you will turn to that student and remind him, "Actually, it is fair. She needs a fidget to be able to concentrate. If you did, we would give you a fidget. But you don't. Later on, when it's time for us to go to music, you're going to be sitting in the back so the noise isn't too loud for you. She won't be, because she doesn't have trouble with loud noises. Remember, fair doesn't mean equal, it means everyone getting what he or she needs."

Finally, in schools that rely on traditional school discipline, the teacher is the problem solver, the one who comes up with the solutions and says how things are going to go. When running a prosocial classroom, you have a lot of other problem solvers available to you, and this works well when using Plan B. In fact, this is especially helpful when you are not sure how to solve a problem yourself. Twenty-five heads are better than one! And, as we discussed earlier, when the students are coauthors of the solution, they are far more likely to be invested.

## PART 3

# SCALING AND SUSTAINING THE SHIFT IN DISCIPLINE

# CHAPTER 12
## SCHOOLWIDE CHANGE AND IMPLEMENTATION

> *Principal Newcomb sits at her desk and looks at the posters*
> *on her wall, which memorialize the various initiatives she*
> *championed in the seven years since she arrived at North*
> *High School. At the beginning, each initiative was exciting*
> *and full of promise, but now she contemplates how much*
> *good they really did. Sure, there were tiny reminders here*
> *and there of all those professional development days, but*
> *was anyone really practicing what they learned? And more*
> *importantly, did anything really change for the 900 students*
> *in the building? Principal Newcomb resolves that the CPS*
> *materials will not gather dust on her teachers' bookshelves*
> *the following year. If they are going to do this, she wants*
> *to do it right.*

During the same time that we have been working with countless schools
across North America and beyond to implement CPS, a new field of
study, called implementation science, has developed. This field has verified what we have learned through lived experience and has contributed much to our thinking and the way we work. In the last two decades
of implementation in schools, we have experienced some great suc-
cesses, some total failures, and everything in between. Reflecting upon
the commonalities when things go well, our observations are consistent
with what implementation scientists have also found across many different types of organizations that implement evidence-based approaches.

If you are looking not only to learn CPS yourself, but to adopt its use across a whole school or district, you will want to adhere to best practices for implementation. While we have seen CPS spread across schools and districts due to the hard work and commitment of a single educator who implemented CPS from the ground up and inspired one teacher at a time, schoolwide adoption of the approach is more likely to go well if you are a school leader or you have the full support of one. In Box 12.1,

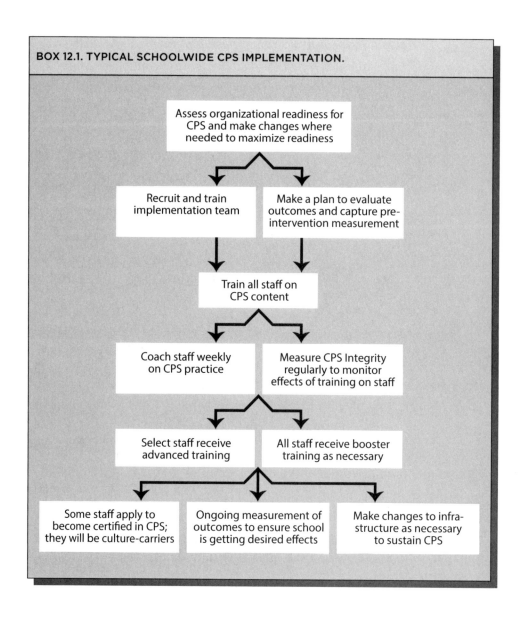

**BOX 12.1. TYPICAL SCHOOLWIDE CPS IMPLEMENTATION.**

Assess organizational readiness for CPS and make changes where needed to maximize readiness

Recruit and train implementation team

Make a plan to evaluate outcomes and capture pre-intervention measurement

Train all staff on CPS content

Coach staff weekly on CPS practice

Measure CPS Integrity regularly to monitor effects of training on staff

Select staff receive advanced training

All staff receive booster training as necessary

Some staff apply to become certified in CPS; they will be culture-carriers

Ongoing measurement of outcomes to ensure school is getting desired effects

Make changes to infra-structure as necessary to sustain CPS

you will see an outline of the typical school implementation process, and then in the remainder of this chapter, we will detail for you what our current process of schoolwide implementation looks like, drawing from both implementation science and our own experiences. These lessons learned can help ensure that all your hard work, time, and resources actually make for sustainable change that will be around long after the initial excitement of any new approach starts to fade.

## TASK #1: ASSESS READINESS FOR CHANGE

Implementing any evidence-based practice (but especially one in which adults must share a common mindset that flies in the face of conventional wisdom) requires changing the behavior of staff as well as the climate, culture, and structures of the school. In other words, it is a substantial undertaking. Inevitably, when you try to implement a new approach, it will seem as if you are shining a bright light on whatever preexisting weaknesses are in the system. Poor morale? Weak communication practices? You won't be able to hide preexisting issues like this. Just be careful that people don't blame CPS for revealing these weaknesses, which will simply become more glaring during the change process as they would when implementing any other highly inidividualized approach to school discipline.

Since change is stressful, school leaders should work with CPS experts to determine whether a system is ready for this kind of change before beginning the implementation process. Scaccia and colleagues (2015) suggest that organizational readiness for change is best measured as the product of three factors: motivation for change, capacity for change in general, and capacity for the specific innovation it will be adopting (they use the heuristic: $R=MC^2$). Motivation for change is the degree to which the staff believe that this change is needed, is possible, and is compatible (or could be) with their current practices. General capacity is the degree to which the staff have the expertise, the time, the resources, and the positive climate necessary to undergo any change process. Innovation-specific capacity is the degree to which the staff have resources necessary for this specific intervention—for instance, in the case of CPS, they will need the time for extensive training and coaching, and there should be a few CPS culture carriers who are leading the way. The goal of a thorough readiness evaluation is not to come to a yes or no decision of whether the system is ready for CPS, but rather to identify areas that may need some attention before you embark on school-wide implementation.

## TASK #2: RECRUIT YOUR TEAM

Implementation science tells us that it is critical to form an implementation team who will be in charge of overseeing the implementation process. The process will go much more quickly and effectively this way (Balas & Boren, 2000; Fixsen et al., 2001). When implementing CPS schoolwide, your team should be small and consist of representation from school leadership as well as other roles in the school building, including, importantly, classroom teachers. The implementation team will want to think about who the likely leaders of implementation will be, because ideally those individuals should receive some training in CPS prior to the rest of the staff, so they have a greater degree of expertise than those who will be learning from them.

## TASK #3: TRAIN YOUR STAFF WELL

Like any other evidence-based practice in a school, successful implementation of CPS depends upon having a comprehensive training plan. All staff members in a building (right down to the support staff in the office if possible) should be exposed to a basic introductory, or exposure, training in the approach. This training will not help attendees get to a level of proficiency in practicing the approach, but it will protect against some basic misconceptions that tend to abound. CPS exposure is also a great way to stimulate healthy dialogue among the staff about what implementation will require from different people in the building, and to cultivate engagement and enthusiasm.

To get staff to a point where they can practice the approach, however, requires more intensive training. Thus, most of your staff, including all classroom teachers, should attend advanced training. We have found that after initial exposure it takes about 15 hours of additional training to get staff to the place where they feel equipped to practice all aspects of the model that have been described in preceding chapters. Ideally, this training takes place during the professional development days just prior to the start of school.

## TASK #4: COACHING IS CRITICAL

Beware! If you set your staff loose to practice CPS with training alone, don't expect much to happen. Joyce and Showers (2002) conducted a study that paints a bleak picture of what can be expected when teachers are trained in a new practice without regular small doses of coaching. They report that, in training a new approach, teaching the theory plus demonstrating the approach resulted in 30 percent of trainees understanding the concept, but none changed what they do to be consistent with the new approach. When trainers added in a chance for trainees to practice the new approach, 60 percent understood the concept, and five percent changed their practice. But when trainers added in coaching sessions, 95 percent of trainees understood the concepts, and 95 percent changed their practice. In essence, the vast majority of professional development dollars may be wasted, because they go toward what we call "spray-and-pray" training, in which a trainer comes to spray a little information over the trainees, and then pray that some of it sticks, with no follow-up. While a good professional development training can pique staff members' interest and increase their knowledge, as we described above, it will not translate into practice without follow-up coaching.

Remember, as we outlined in Chapter 8, to build new connections in the brain one needs to have adequate dosing and spacing as well as practice in real-life situations. This is true of the adult brain as well. Building new skills in educators requires changing their brains. This is why one long, uninterrupted training dose is unlikely to be as effective as small, repetitive, regular doses of training and practice spaced out over time. More specifically, when we implement CPS in a school, coaching involves having staff meet in small groups, on a weekly basis, with a CPS Certified Trainer, to discuss students and their attempts to apply CPS. The coach assesses their documentation (e.g., CPS-APT) and assessment and planning practices, and the group listens to group members' recordings of Plan B conversations, while discussing and rating fidelity or adherence to CPS using the CPS Integrity Scorecard (see Appendix C). This coaching process should take place weekly, immediately following the intensive training, and continue throughout the first year of schoolwide implementation. During that process, natural leaders will start to emerge. These are the staff who are passionate about and skilled with the approach. They are the staff whom you want to become the culture carriers within your building. After participating in weekly coaching for at least six months, those leaders should receive another 15 hours of training. This extra training helps them to become more proficient, not only in troubleshooting their own work, but also the work of their colleagues, allowing them to be a local resource for all the staff in the school.

After completing the second round of intensive training, staff are eligible to apply to become certified in CPS. The certification process is highly individualized, is completed through distance learning, and is intended to help participants achieve a high level of proficiency in applying the approach. Once staff are certified in CPS, they can apply to become certified as CPS trainers, which will allow them to conduct formal CPS training within their school system. Having staff who are certified in CPS and having internal CPS trainers are important for a school's CPS sustainability. Developing your own in-house CPS trainers means that you will be able to provide CPS training for all new staff, refresher training to reenergize existing staff and prevent drift, and coaching as well. Implementation science tells us it takes two to four years to fully implement an evidence-based practice in a school because in order to fully implement, you must produce a sustainable practice. This has been our own experience with CPS as well. You can make many of these changes in a short period of time, but it will be unlikely that those changes remain five years later without this focus on important aspects of good implementation, such as certification for your culture carriers.

## TASK #5: MEASURE AND MONITOR CPS INTEGRITY AND OUTCOMES

CPS integrity, also called CPS fidelity, is the degree to which CPS is being practiced the way it was intended. If the goal is to increase CPS integrity, it is important to be able to measure it. We have developed a number of CPS integrity tools that allow the implementation team to monitor how implementation is going. One such tool can be found in Appendix C, and we make updated versions available on our website. As mentioned above, these tools can be used to rate fidelity of practice via monitoring documentation (like CPS-APTs), reviewing recordings of Plan B conversations, and observing practice more generally. Findings from implementation science suggest that a good benchmark for implementation is achieved when 60 percent of staff in a school building are using the approach with reasonable fidelity (Alexander, 2011).

In addition to monitoring CPS integrity, it is important also to evaluate outcomes to know whether high integrity implementation is indeed producing the results you were hoping for. As we'll see in Chapter 15, there have been an increasing number of research studies on CPS published in education and mental health journals. However, monitoring outcomes is not reserved only for those doing academic research studies. Even if you do not plan to be contributing to the generalizable research on CPS, it will be important for you to evaluate the impact of the approach in your system. Results of these evaluations should feed back into the implementation process to help you know who may need more support, and in what areas.

So how do you decide what outcomes to measure? The first step is thinking about why you implemented CPS in the first place. Was it to reduce challenging behaviors or disciplinary referrals? If so, you will want to assess these student-focused outcomes. Was it to build cognitive skills in your students? You could use the Likert scale version of our

Thinking Skills Inventory (TSI) to measure these. Or was it to reduce teacher stress or shift the mindset of teachers to a more compassionate place? If so, you will want to think about using measures intended to tap these specific domains, like our CPS Adherence and Impact Measure (CPS-AIM).

## TASK #6: MAKE CHANGES TO INFRASTRUCTURE

Once a critical mass of people in the building are practicing CPS with integrity, it becomes time to cast an eye toward other systemic issues that will need to be attended to if the approach will be sustainable. Tensions will naturally arise between existing structures and roles and what staff are now being asked to do using CPS. For example, some aspects of CPS may conflict with other approaches that were used in the school building prior. There may be policies or procedures, as well as structures to meetings and documentation, that no longer fit with the way staff are trying to approach school discipline. As these tensions arise, there will be an opportunity to examine them, to ensure that CPS becomes embedded in all aspects of the system. For example, most schools have some forum to gather the educators involved with any particular challenging student in order to develop a coherent behavior intervention plan. However, the people invited to the meeting, the language used during the meeting, the paperwork completed at the meeting, and the overall focus may be inconsistent with CPS. Slowly but surely, you'll want to collaboratively rethink all those aspects, and how you can effectively embed CPS into as many areas as possible. In Chapter 13, we highlight some of the most predictable tensions that arise during the change process, and give examples of how you can put the model itself to work to help address them.

# CHAPTER 13
## NO PAIN, NO GAIN: COMMON CHALLENGES

*At the end of his introductory training in CPS, Superintendent Langdon sat thinking about the ways CPS was, and wasn't, relevant to his role. "After teaching for 23 years, I don't work directly with the students anymore," he thought. "My issues are more with the adults in our buildings—the parents, teachers, and my fellow administrators. I feel like we could all use a dose of this. I wonder if we could use CPS with each other?"*

As we discussed in Chapter 12, shifting the culture of an entire school while implementing a highly individualized form of school discipline is bound to put all aspects of the system under a microscope. A bright light will shine on any preexisting weaknesses in that system. In addition, the system will be challenged to improve many of the ways staff have been going about business. In the last two decades, implementing CPS in schools of all kinds, we have found that there are some common, almost inevitable challenges that arise when implementing CPS. In this chapter, we will discuss the most common challenges and some of the ways we have found to address them. You might not be surprised to learn that a key theme has always been the importance of trying to solve those problems collaboratively.

### LEADING THROUGH CHANGE

Transforming school discipline means changing the way the adults in the building think and act, and that change can be painful. We learned in Chapter 8, though, that manageable doses of good stress are required to change the brain. The same is true of systems. Recall the old saying: "No pain, no gain." If the system isn't experiencing any distress, you can rest assured that no fundamental change is happening. However, if you move too quickly and there is too much distress in the system, you will set things back further than when you started. Thus, one of the most important jobs of any leader in a school is to titrate the amount of pain that staff feel at one time. As a leader, you want to make sure there is some discomfort, but not too much (Heifetz, 1994).

To titrate the pain, you will need to pace your expectations for how people use the approach. In the very beginning, you'll want to make sure staff are trying their hand at the assessment process, with the goal of facilitating a shift in mindset. In this way, you are simply asking people to think differently, to see challenging behavior through the lens of a lack of skill rather than a lack of will, but not to behave very differently. Once people's mindsets are starting to shift, you can then slowly increase the discomfort a little more by having staff reflect on the limitations of existing disciplinary strategies when it comes to addressing skill deficits. Simultaneously, you can encourage staff to think about when they might have chosen a different option, such as when they could have tried Plan C instead of Plan A. And finally, you begin to state the expectation that staff will start to try Plan B conversations, providing plenty of feedback, coaching, and support through the initial struggles (which are inevitable). But even the best of implementation plans will not protect you from what are bound to be some significant setbacks along the way. Don't worry if you need to take a few steps back and reduce the demands on staff if things become a little too tense. Once everyone is re-regulated, you can move forward again.

## STAFF BUY-IN

Because the CPS approach to differentiated discipline represents a major shift in thinking, it is not uncommon for educators—like other adults—to have some reservations and concerns about the process. If you are passionate about the philosophy of CPS, ironically, you may be at higher risk for trying to use Plan A with your colleagues who don't share this philosophy. Being incredibly passionate about this approach ourselves, and wanting everyone to embrace it, we can speak firsthand to the frustration when others don't, and how tempting it is to impose Collaborative Problem Solving on others. However, we can also speak firsthand to the limitations of doing it this way. What we have learned is, however hard you try, you can't use Plan A to get your colleagues to do Plan B. It may not surprise you to hear that when someone has concerns about this shift in thinking and disciplinary strategy, we recommend that you listen hard to what their concerns are, and take some time to really understand where they're coming from, before sharing the reasons you are eager to pursue this new line of thinking (i.e., your concerns or perspective), and then—you guessed it—invite them to think together with you about how to move forward given the perspectives that each of you hold.

When it comes to helping shift the mindset of your colleagues to embrace the philosophy behind CPS, it can be useful to remember that in the beginning, while resisting the urge to impose your will with Plan A, it is okay to be a bit of a salesperson. But one of the oldest adages of sales is helpful here: Know your customer. Let's imagine your family walks into a showroom looking at new cars. Your partner wants to know about the safety ratings. You want to know how much it costs. Your son, who will be driving soon, is interested in how much horsepower the car has. Your younger daughter wants to know whether there are cup holders in the back. If the salesperson is going to make the sale, he or she will need to appeal to what matters most to each person.

Like the members of your family in that scenario, you will find that different colleagues care about different things. True to the spirit of Plan B, your first goal is to listen hard and ask questions so you know what any particular colleague cares about. Some educators simply want to put an end to the challenging behavior so they can get back to teaching the other students. Others are more concerned about getting an expectation met today and then not waking up to the same old problem day in and day out. Others are up to the challenge of dealing with daily difficulties, as long as their students are developing the skills they need to be successful in the future. Still others are primarily concerned about the relationship they have with their students. Recall that these are precisely the five goals that we discussed in Chapter 5, and Plan B is the only one of your three options that can work toward all those goals simultaneously. Once you understand which of these goals matter the most to your colleagues, you'll be in a good position to "sell" the merits of CPS. Fortunately, it is also often easier to embrace the role of salesperson when you remember that what you are selling is a more accurate, humane and compassionate way to think about, and approach, students.

As you try to address the challenging behaviors that arise when teachers are resistant to CPS, watch out for the particularly clever educator who suggests that by telling staff that they should be using CPS, you are using Plan A. Remember that choosing CPS as your approach to school discipline and asking staff to practice the approach is not Plan A. It is simply setting clear expectations. Any leader in a school building should be setting clear expectations. Just as there are expectations for which academic curricula will be used, there should be expectations for how staff are expected to handle challenging behaviors. Now what if you go ahead and set those clear expectations about using CPS, but certain staff don't use the approach? Then you have an unmet expectation, or what we might call a Problem! Recall that you have three options for handling problems, and ultimately Plan B is likely to be your most successful option to try to get your expectations met while also addressing the concerns of that staff member. This is important because if one of your colleagues is not embracing the approach, he probably has good concerns, and he is unlikely to adopt CPS unless his concerns are addressed. School leaders who practice the CPS that they preach will find successful implementation a whole lot easier.

Some of the most important Plan B that will happen in your school will likely be without any student in sight. Most schools that have successfully implemented CPS can in fact point to crucial moments when there were disagreements among the staff about how to handle particular disciplinary issues, and someone modeled the process of Plan B right then and there. Just be careful, because as you start asking questions, reflecting your colleagues' concerns, and reassuring them that you're not trying to impose your perspective on them, they will likely ask you if you are trying to use Plan B with them! To which you can happily reply, "Yes I am!"

## FINDING THE TIME

Plan B can be an effective way to handle what looks like resistance but typically are valid concerns, and it can also help to break down barriers that impede the process of implementation. One of the most common barriers in schools is finding the time to use CPS. While logically we may understand that taking the time to have a five-minute Plan B conversation with a student now may save hours of addressing and readdressing a chronic problem in the classroom over the remainder of the school year, time can still be a very practical barrier to implementation. Remember, Plan B with staff can be a transparent process, with no secret steps or agenda. Let's listen in on this conversation from a particular elementary school that was an early adopter of CPS, and that could have occurred in just about any school in which we've ever worked.

MR. CARTER: I actually really like the idea of Plan B. I love the idea of listening to my students and building relationships with them. But I just don't think it's realistic. I mean, I have 27 students in my class. I just don't have time to do Plan B with every student all day long.

ASSISTANT PRINCIPAL SHEFKSI: All right, I hear you. So you're saying there's a lot you like about Plan B, but you're worried that it's not feasible. You don't think you have the time to do it (*reflective listening*).

**MR. CARTER:** I've barely got time to breathe, let alone pull kids aside to do problem solving.

**ASSISTANT PRINCIPAL SHEFKSI:** So your days are jam packed, and you're not able to imagine when you would have an in-depth conversation with a student (*reflective listening*). Am I hearing you right?

**MR. CARTER:** Well, I could carve out the time to do it, but then something else will have to give. Either I won't be able to do my lesson planning, or the rest of the class is going to miss out on learning time, or they will get off task or something. And I know that, theoretically, I am supposed to do it at lunch or before school. But I don't even take lunch, and the students I need to do Plan B with aren't at school early!

**ASSISTANT PRINCIPAL SHEFKSI:** Ah. The idea of doing Plan B when the students are not in class doesn't seem possible. And you'd love to do it when the students are engaged in something else, but someone would have to be supervising them so they don't get off task (*reflective listening*).

**MR. CARTER:** Exactly!

**ASSISTANT PRINCIPAL SHEFKSI:** I hear you loud and clear. You'd like to do Plan B, but don't feel you have the time. (*Moves to the second step.*) And I'm worried that these chronic behavioral difficulties are actually making it even harder for you, sapping even more instructional time in the long run. (*Moves to the third step.*) So I wonder if there's something we can do so that you have time for Plan B aimed at decreasing the chronic behavioral problems you are dealing with—without compromising other important things or causing the other students to miss out or get off task. What do you think? Any ideas?

**MR. CARTER:** Well, if I had any brilliant ideas, I would have tried them by now. I think if we had more time from one of the guidance counselors, like Chandra, she'd be able to take this on.

**ASSISTANT PRINCIPAL SHEFKSI:** You mean Chandra would have the problem-solving conversations?

**MR. CARTER:** Yes!

**ASSISTANT PRINCIPAL SHEFKSI** *(following the script and testing the solution out)*: That's one idea. I can see how Chandra would have more time to do it, and you'd be teaching the rest of the class. I guess my concern about that is that she's not necessarily going to know what happened in the first place or be there to help enact the solution. But I think you're on to something. I like this idea of getting more hands on deck.

**MR. CARTER:** There's no way I can do this alone.

**ASSISTANT PRINCIPAL SHEFKSI:** I wonder if we could use Chandra to help, but still allow you to be the one doing Plan B.

**MR. CARTER:** Well, if she wants to cover my class while I have a Plan B conversation, it's fine by me!

**ASSISTANT PRINCIPAL SHEFKSI:** That's an interesting idea. It would keep your class on task and give you the time for problem solving. We could discuss that with her, or I'd be happy to cover your class for the few minutes it takes to do Plan B. What do you think of that as a possibility?

**MR. CARTER:** Sure, if you have the time.

**ASSISTANT PRINCIPAL SHEFKSI:** Well, I don't necessarily have tons of time either, but partially that's because of all the students being sent to my office *(laughs)*! So it's worth the time to me. How about if you and I plan out your first Proactive Plan B conversation, so you can have it while I cover your class this afternoon?

**MR. CARTER:** Okay, I'm willing to give it a try.

## COMMUNICATION AND DOCUMENTATION STRUCTURES

Yet another almost inevitable challenge to successful implementation involves communication and documentation. We have never worked with a school that has remarked that implementation of CPS may be a challenge, "but at least we have enough time to talk about students, we always have the right people in the room, we focus on the right stuff, and our documentation is clear!" Communication structures and documentation practices almost always need to be enhanced or reshaped to successfully facilitate the implementation of CPS. Any highly individualized approach to discipline will require good communication and documentation, just in the same way that highly individualized instruction does.

Following are some questions you can ask in order to know whether your structures and practices are strong enough to handle this change:

- Is there a regular forum to discuss students with behavioral challenges and make effective intervention plans?
- Do those meetings regularly involve classroom teachers, the people who have the data regarding problems and skill struggles, and who will be there when the problems happen again?
- Is there a mechanism to communicate solutions that are devised between student support meetings?
- Do your school's Functional Behavior Assessment (FBA) or other behavior intervention forms allow for a place to assess skill struggles?
- Is there documentation to rapidly disseminate the behavior intervention plan to all the teachers who interface with that student? E.g., if the team decides on Plan C for a certain problem, how is everyone apprised of that?

Remember that simply imposing new structures and practices on the team will be less helpful than engaging the team in a collaborative process so they are coauthors adapting existing procedures to meet the needs of the team.

## NEW ROLES AND GOALS

When you're rethinking school discipline, individuals' roles in the building and the goals they are trying to achieve might shift also. For example, a classroom teacher may begin to take the lead role when it comes to using Plan B with a student whom she used to send down to the office for discipline. On the flip side, the school social worker used to be the one managing the students who got dysregulated at school, but all of a sudden, rather than inheriting the dysregulated students when teachers have used Plan A, he might concentrate more on facilitating classroom teachers using Plan B. In the inevitable reshuffling of roles, a premium is placed on teamwork. CPS, or any other highly individualized approach for that matter, requires teammates in different roles to assist and complement each other. Traditional school discipline can often be carried out in isolation, but CPS requires coordination and teamwork. The good news is that, as we described, the process of using Plan B among the adults helps build the kinds of relationships that form the basis of the most effective teams (Ablon, 2018).

When it comes time to think about behavior goals for a student, whether formally registered on an Individualized Education Program (IEP) or simply for internal purposes, the team might need to rethink the typical areas of focus. Perhaps the goals don't just focus on compliance and reducing oppositional behavior, but also on the growth of neuro-cognitive skills in the five domains described in Chapter 4. The team might decide to use the list of skills on the CPS-APT (see Appendix A) to measure progress for a student and even insert those items into the student's IEP goals. Similarly, rather than just setting the goal of reducing challenging behavior, the list of Problems on the CPS-APT becomes the primary indicator of whether the behavior intervention plan is proving successful.

### "BUT THAT'S THE WAY WE'VE ALWAYS DONE IT HERE"

Another predictable challenge is one we refer to as *organizational inertia*. We humans don't like distress. Working in a school is stressful enough, and trying to make change is even harder. For these reasons, the status quo often continues, even if it's not especially effective. As a school gets deeper into the implementation process of CPS, you may find that you begin to question some of the existing policies and procedures that have been in place for a long time and are inconsistent with the philosophy or practice of CPS. You may find yourself limited in using Plan B because of Plan A rules. In those instances, you may need to challenge the rigidity of the system itself. Once again, thankfully, the structure and steps of Plan B provide a road map for doing just that. Rigid rules were probably put in place to address important concerns. The rule is that students can't wear hats and hoodies. The rule is that students must enter and exit through only that door. What are the concerns those rules were put in place to address? For a student who is having a hard time meeting those expectations, there may be more responsive, flexible, and ultimately effective ways to meet the needs of your most challenging students and still address those schoolwide concerns.

Believe it or not, the process of implementation can even call into question the physical spaces of the school and how you make use of them. Could the classroom be set up in order to allow for semiprivate Plan B conversations without students feeling as though all their peers are listening in? Does the vice principal's office create a welcoming environment where everyone feels safe to express their concerns freely? In the most severe examples, isolation rooms may become sensory spaces, with sterile walls and floors replaced by soothing colors and beanbags.

## FLAVOR OF THE YEAR

With great pressure to innovate in our schools, it can be enticing to take on a new evidence-based practice (EBP) every year. However, as we described earlier, it can take two to four years before you have successfully implemented an EBP with fidelity and sustainability. So before taking on any new approach, CPS included, you'll want to think about where you are with other initiatives, and whether those will blend well with CPS. Some of this can be assessed during an evaluation of your organization's readiness for change (see Chapter 12). But be prepared for some challenges to ensue, even with the most compatible practices. Clearly, if an approach is not aligned with the philosophy behind CPS, implementation will be limited at best. However, even with philosophically-consonant approaches, each approach has its own language and procedures. Be careful not to have your staff feel awash in EBPs, unsure which approach to use, when, and with whom (this is sometimes called *model fatigue*). If there are concerns about the integration of existing models, that's a good time to gather around the problem-solving table. Fortunately, some of the most common existing structures used in schools today fit hand-in-glove with CPS.

## THE FIT WITH EXISTING INITIATIVES

Whether a school is looking to overhaul school discipline entirely or a particular educator wants to try a different approach to discipline within her own class, the process does not occur within a vacuum. Most schools have existing disciplinary systems and models of intervention for students who struggle, whether academically, socially, emotionally, or behaviorally. Therefore, a critical aspect of implementing any new approach is ensuring that it can be integrated successfully with other current initiatives in the building or district. While CPS is an evidence-based approach that provides schools a blueprint for better understanding and helping students with behavioral challenges, as discussed above, it is not simply a tool or technique, and it is way more than just Plan B. CPS is a mentality and a process that is not meant to be a standalone practice. So in fact CPS *should* be integrated with other existing evidence-based initiatives commonly practiced in schools.

Multi-Tiered Systems of Support (MTSS) is a best practice for creating safe and successful schools, and CPS complements many common MTSSs currently practiced in schools, such as Response to Intervention (RTI) and Positive Behavioral Interventions and Supports (PBIS). RTI proactively identifies students at risk by systematically tracking their progress to ensure that they receive the degree of necessary support and intervention, from Tier 1 (high-quality classroom instruction, screening, and group interventions) and Tier 2 (targeted interventions) through Tier 3 (intensive interventions and comprehensive evaluation). PBIS provides a framework for teaching behavioral expectations to all students and provides supports and interventions in the form of schoolwide policies and procedures. Through PBIS, a school identifies Tier 1, 2, and 3 supports. However, PBIS alone is not intended to adequately address the needs of the one to 15 percent of students who do not respond to schoolwide interventions and who require much more individualized and specialized intervention. CPS provides the Tier 3 interventions for these high-risk, high-need students identified through RTI or PBIS (while also promoting a safer and more collaborative environment that benefits all students). In addition, the CPS assessment procedures described in Chapters 3 and 4 can also be integrated with any MTSS to help identify when students are lagging in their development of neurocognitive skills and in need of more support, as well as to track progress after intervention.

Another example of fit with other school initiatives includes the integration of restorative practices and CPS. The primary principles of restorative practices are consistent with CPS: Justice requires working to repair harm that has been caused; those involved and affected should participate in the response; positive relationships and empathy are crucial; and punitive interventions are counterproductive. Instead of simply punishing and labeling youth who have committed crimes, both CPS and restorative practices give youth the opportunity to take responsibility for their behavior, understand the full impact of their actions on others, and repair harm done to victims. Restorative practices, however, through restorative circles, provide a crucial framework for involving the entire community, whereas CPS emphasizes more individual and small group intervention that focuses on skill building. In this way, the effects of implementing restorative practices and CPS are additive.

Thanks in large part to the Adverse Childhood Experiences (ACE) Study (Felitti et al., 1998) and the important work that has followed, schools these days are much more aware of the prevalence and impact of chronic stress and trauma on students' ability to learn and behave. Most schools aspire to adopt trauma-informed or trauma-sensitive approaches when it comes to meeting the needs of their most challenging students. Ironically, those are the students who are most often on the receiving end of traditional school discipline. Why is that ironic? Because, as we discussed in Chapter 8, traditional school discipline relies on mechanisms of power and control to change students' behavior, which is the opposite of providing trauma-informed care. The use of power and control is thought to be re-traumatizing and to cause developmental damage. The challenge is that there is no single approach frequently adopted by schools that makes the educational setting more trauma-sensitive. In our experience, educators are eager to embrace the ideals and principles of trauma-sensitive care, but end up feeling adrift when it comes to what to do to put those principles into practice. Fortunately, one of the most exciting developments in recent years related to CPS has been the growing awareness that it represents a practical solution to providing trauma-informed care, once educators are aware of the devastating impact of chronic stress and trauma on the brain (Perry & Ablon, 2014). Plan A uses the power differential to try to induce compliance, but with traumatized students, a power differential causes dysregulation and dissociation. One goal of trauma-informed care is to reduce the power differential, which is what you are doing when you shift from Plan A to Plan B, and the student's concerns become every bit as important as yours. Being trauma-sensitive involves giving the student a sense of control without sole responsibility for the process. Again, the framework of Plan B provides a road map for doing just that. If you adhere to everything we've discussed in this book so far, you will actually have come a long way toward being a trauma-sensitive school.

Finally, Carol Dweck's (2006) book, *Mindset*, and Angela Duckworth's (2016) book, *Grit*, have had a significant impact on schools across North America. In *Mindset*, Dweck describes the difference between a fixed- versus growth mindset. With a fixed mindset, a student believes his intelligence and talent are fixed traits that lead to success. If a child does not believe he possesses these traits, he is likely to give up easily in the face of frustration or difficulty. On the contrary, a student with a growth mindset believes his abilities can improve and grow over time through trying different strategies and approaches when challenged, combined with sustained effort. Dweck explains that a growth mindset is fostered when educators praise a student's effort and strategies, not just the outcomes. CPS is quite consistent with the ideas behind fostering a growth mindset. The philosophy introduces the notion that if a student is not doing well, we should figure out how to develop the skills she lacks so that she can do better. The natural process of generating and testing out solutions, reevaluating and revising them as needed, is exactly the kind of process that facilitates growth.

Similarly, in *Grit*, Duckworth discusses the benefits of perseverance, which can only be fostered if one believes that skills can grow and problems can be solved. The theories of growth mindset, grit, and CPS all focus on fostering intrinsic drive, and are based on the idea of building skills. Thus, not only is CPS consonant with the theories of growth mindset and grit, but if your school is working hard to adopt a growth mindset with your most challenging students, CPS can help.

In summary, you can feel optimistic about integrating CPS into your current school initiatives as long as they are philosophically aligned. This is good news because the approach also fills an important gap when it comes meeting the needs of the most vulnerable and challenging students, who need highly individualized, specialized intervention.

# CHAPTER 14

# PLAN B WITH COLLEAGUES AND PARENTS

*Vice Principal Shaw shuffles through the folder in front of him as the meeting begins. "When we look at the situations in which Ava seems to be struggling the most, it seems like it is primarily in science class," he says. "That must be where her inflexibility is causing the most trouble."*

*"Well, if we are being perfectly honest," says the school guidance counselor tentatively, "flexibility isn't exactly our science teacher's strong suit, either. I think there may be a few reasons Ava is doing much better in everyone else's class."*

There are many different ways that school leaders can help foster the mindset and practice of CPS with their staff. The most fundamental way is by embracing the notion that *educators are doing the best they can with the skills they have.* If a staff member is struggling with any of the expectations in front of her, a Plan B leader will assume skill, not will, is interfering, and will work hard not only to identify the staff member's concerns and make sure they get addressed, but also to help that staff member develop her own skills.

In many cases, once staff have become familiar with the five skill domains on which we focus, they can't help but reflect upon their own skills, and often even make disclosures to each other about those with which they feel they struggle. This will provide an opportunity to remind the staff that everybody in the building, including students, staff, and administrators, has their own strengths and weaknesses. And the job of a good mentor is to help staff develop skills. Schools that have fully embraced CPS sometimes embed self-assessment of the five categories of skills in annual reviews. A supervisor can take the opportunity to reflect with a supervisee on which skills that supervisee is hoping to practice and develop during the school year.

The structure of Plan B also provides a great template for coming up with solutions to problems that a staff member may have. By following the structure of Plan B, the school leader does not position herself as the one with all the answers. Rather, she fosters the notion that good leaders ask the right questions and bring together the skills of her team to solve complicated problems (Heifetz, 1994). This kind of problem solving leads to a sense of shared leadership where everyone owns the problems confronting the school.

## EDUCATORS DO THE BEST THEY CAN WITH THE SKILLS THEY HAVE

As we described in Chapter 13, the Plan B process can be helpful for managing resistance to implementation, or addressing barriers to implementation. It can also be helpful for department heads, team leaders, and administrators to conduct general management and supervision within a school. Just like students, staff members may not always meet the expectations of administrators. (And administrators may not always meet the expectations of their staff). In fact, in response to expectations, you may see staff exhibit challenging behaviors of their own: avoidance, refusal, and even backtalk. Ms. Wilson owed you final grades yesterday but didn't get them in; now she turns and walks the other way when she sees you coming. Multiple teachers report that Mr. Barta was telling everyone in the staff room that he won't be staying to the end of the professional development day, as you asked of everyone.

When events like this occur, you have a problem to solve. So what do you do? First, remind yourself that *educators are doing the best they can with the skills they have*; there must be a reasonable concern and a lagging skill getting in the way of that staff member meeting your expectation, and the challenging behavior you see is her best attempt to deal with the problem. Then, you will do the same thing you do with students who aren't meeting your expectations: You have three options; decide which one you want to use. Sure, you could threaten disciplinary action (Plan A) or decide that you will focus your attention elsewhere (Plan C), but there are clear advantages to Plan B. Let's listen in on a conversation with Mrs. Howard, who hasn't attended the required CPS coaching group in three weeks.

> **PRINCIPAL KELLY:** Hey, Liz, it's been a while since I saw you in our CPS coaching group. Can you fill me in?
>
> **MRS. HOWARD:** Well, things have been pretty good; I just haven't felt the need to go.
>
> **PRINCIPAL KELLY:** I'm glad things are going well. And at the same time, it's hard for me to imagine that you haven't been seeing any behavior problems, especially considering the high-needs students you have.
>
> **MRS. HOWARD:** Well, that's true.
>
> **PRINCIPAL KELLY:** So I wonder if there's something else that might be getting in the way. I'm not trying to give you a hard time; I really want to understand (*reassurance*).
>
> **MRS. HOWARD:** Okay, the truth? I've been teaching for 23 years, and I feel pretty good about my ability to teach. The last thing I want to do at this point in my career is try something that will make me look like a fool.
>
> **PRINCIPAL KELLY:** What do you mean?
>
> **MRS. HOWARD:** I have been trying the Plan B thing, but I don't want others in the CPS coaching group critiquing my videos and saying that I don't know what I'm doing, when I'm not exactly new to the profession.
>
> **PRINCIPAL KELLY:** Got it. So you're saying you're not averse to trying Plan B, you just don't want to look foolish, or as if you don't know what you're doing, to others (*reflective listening*).
>
> **MRS. HOWARD:** That's basically it.
>
> **PRINCIPAL KELLY:** That makes sense, and I appreciate your honesty. I

think a lot of people would agree with you that no one wants to look like they don't know what they are doing, especially in front of less experienced folks (*reassurance*). And I do know people look to you to know what they should be doing in the building, considering your experience. (*Moves to the second step.*) One of my concerns is that if you're not doing it, others may not either. And as the school leader, it's important to me that we get the community on the same page by all practicing and learning this approach together. So I bet . . .

MRS. HOWARD *(smirking)*: You bet there's a way that we get both our concerns met?

PRINCIPAL KELLY: See? You're better at this than you thought! Yes, I bet there's a way that you don't have to look like a fool in front of others, and you are still practicing and learning this new approach and setting the example for others. Any ideas?

MRS. HOWARD: Well, we are required to submit the video recordings of our attempts at Plan B conversations for our coaching sessions. I can't think of a way that others won't see me struggle before I'm good at it.

PRINCIPAL KELLY: So having the whole group watching your videos doesn't sound like it can be part of the solution. And I suppose it doesn't have to be. But without that, how can would you get feedback so you continue to improve?

MRS. HOWARD: Well, what if our CPS coach watches my videos in advance and provides feedback during the coaching session, without everyone watching the whole thing? I guess if I knew we could do that, I'd be willing to give it a shot.

PRINCIPAL KELLY: And you won't feel like a fool if it's only the coach watching the video?

MRS. HOWARD: No, I don't mind the coach seeing me struggle with this. Only the newer teachers.

PRINCIPAL KELLY: And then you'll be taking part in this important schoolwide initiative, and others will see you are on board. It sounds like that would address both our concerns. This sounds like a great plan. Maybe once we have some videos of you doing great Plan B you can even show those to the younger teachers as a model.

As you can see, not only does Plan B provide a good structure for handling problems with staff, but it also has the benefit of leading by example.

## PARENTS DO THE BEST THEY CAN, TOO!

So what if you are doing great CPS at school, but the student goes home to Plan A parents who subscribe to conventional wisdom? Will all your hard work be undone? We get asked this question a lot when we train educators. The interesting thing is that we get the same question when we train parents, just in reverse: Will their hard work at home get undone by all the conventional discipline at school? In either case, we like to remind folks of the fact that *educators are doing the best they can with the skills they have* and *so are parents*! CPS provides a blameless understanding of challenging behavior and a framework for dealing with it that can be shared by the adults in the child's life. As we will discuss in Chapter 15, CPS is one of few approaches that provide a common philosophy, language, and process that not only can be applied across settings, but has demonstrated effectiveness across them.

In our experience, the number one barrier to enlisting parental collaboration with behavioral challenges at school is conventional wisdom. We have never met a parent of a challenging student who walks into school not having felt blamed for their child's behavior at some point in the past. So you will likely need to go overboard to show parents that you do not subscribe to conventional wisdom. How? By telling them just that!

> *"Just so you know, we don't believe that nonsense about parents being to blame for their kids' challenging behavior. Around here, we realize every student is working on something. Some students struggle with certain academic issues and need support. Other students struggle with behavior and need support for that. In fact, parents whose kids struggle with their*

*behavior have to work much harder than parents with easy kids! So you won't be blamed here. We have great empathy. We also don't believe it's the student's fault. Kids are doing the best they can with the skills they have! And we know that kids with challenging behavior are working harder than anyone else to control their behavior."*

A quick explanation like that can go a long way toward setting parents' minds at ease and paving the way for them to be a part of the team collaborating to help the student and the educators. Many teachers and administrators describe unpleasant interactions with parents as among the most stressful parts of their jobs. So what do you do about particularly challenging parents to deal with? You guessed it! Remember, they lack skill, not will. Approach them with empathy and understanding, and put Plan B to work in your interactions with them. Let's listen in on a school team discussing how they have been struggling to enlist Jaylynn's mom's help with some recent challenges they have had with Jaylynn, who is a 3rd grade student in a collaborative school for youth who need special education services.

> **ASSISTANT PRINCIPAL:** Okay, we're here to make a plan for working with Jaylynn. Mrs. Cooper, can you describe what's been going on in the classroom?
>
> **MRS. COOPER:** Since the beginning of the year, we've been having trouble getting Jaylynn to meet any of our expectations. The biggest challenge is anything having to do with homework.
>
> **GUIDANCE COUNSELOR:** Well, I know for sure that this is a home where there is a lot going on. I'm not sure whether there is any adult supervision around homework.
>
> **MRS. COOPER:** That has been my concern, too; every time I open up her backpack in the morning, it hasn't been touched since it left school the day before. It seems to me that some of the work that needs to be done is with Jaylynn's mom!
>
> **ASSISTANT PRINCIPAL:** Okay, but let's start by remembering that moms are doing the best they can with the skills they have. We're all

working on something, right? So, what is it that we think Jaylynn's mom may be struggling with here?

**MRS. COOPER:** I think it may have to do with organizational skills and planning. She certainly seems to have a hard time staying on top of Jaylynn's homework and school forms.

**GUIDANCE COUNSELOR:** I suspect you're right about that. And from what I can tell, she's juggling a lot of things.

**MRS. COOPER:** So how do we make her take responsibility for prioritizing her daughter's education?

**ASSISTANT PRINCIPAL:** Well, I would vote for using Plan B instead of Plan A here. I doubt we will have much success *making* her do something that is probably hard for reasons we may not completely understand. I'd be happy to participate in that conversation with Jaylynn's mom.

**MRS. COOPER:** That sounds good to me—except I doubt you'll ever get her in here. That's part of the problem. She just doesn't seem to care about how Jaylynn is doing in school.

**ASSISTANT PRINCIPAL:** I know it feels that way because she hasn't been particularly involved, but again, let's remember she's probably doing the best she can to handle what's going on right now for them, with the skills she brings to the table. I bet she would want to be doing the best by Jaylynn if she could. What do you think the barriers are to her meeting with us?

**MRS. COOPER:** When I asked her to come in and talk, she gave me an earful about how she can't miss work or else she would get fired.

**GUIDANCE COUNSELOR:** I can reach out to her and see if there's a better time for her.

*(Later in the week, early in the morning before drop-off)* . . .

**GUIDANCE COUNSELOR:** Thanks for coming in so early, Ms. Jordan.

**MS. JORDAN:** I only have a few minutes so I'm not late for work. To be honest, I'm not happy about being here—dealing with Jaylynn is your job. That's why I send her to school.

**MRS. COOPER:** Well, one of the things we want to talk about is homework. We can't fix that all by ourselves. That part is your responsibility.

**ASSISTANT PRINCIPAL:** Let's slow down here a bit. First thing I want to acknowledge is how much we enjoy having Jaylynn in our school. She's a great friend to her peers, and we all love her creativity. Now, there are some things she's working on, just like every other student in the building. And I want to be clear that we don't think those things are anybody's fault; certainly not yours, Ms. Jordan. We know that you want the best for your daughter as well (*reassurance*). So let's take the homework issue. Can you help us understand what's going on, Ms. Jordan?

**MS. JORDAN:** I hope you're not about to tell me that it's my job to make sure she does her homework! I've already got two jobs, and I don't even get home until she's in bed!

**ASSISTANT PRINCIPAL:** Got it. That's really helpful for us to know. Sounds like you have an awful lot on your plate! Is Jaylynn alone most afternoons, or with someone else (*clarifying question*)?

**MS. JORDAN:** I don't leave my nine-year-old alone, if that's what you're trying to say!

**ASSISTANT PRINCIPAL:** Sorry, I didn't mean to suggest that. I was just trying to understand what's happening with Jaylynn during the time we might expect her to be working on homework.

**MS. JORDAN:** My neighbor watches her, but I can't tell her that she has to work on homework. She's doing me a favor by watching Jaylynn, and I can't afford to lose her.

**ASSISTANT PRINCIPAL:** Don't worry, we're not saying you have to tell your neighbor to take care of it. We're just trying to understand so we can make a plan together (*reassurance*). If I hear you correctly, it sounds like Jaylynn isn't quite ready to do the homework on her own, but we don't have great options for people to help her get started after school. Is that right (*reflective listening*)?

**MS. JORDAN:** That's about it. And I'm not sure what else I can do.

**ASSISTANT PRINCIPAL** *(moving to second step to try to get at Mrs. Cooper's concerns)*: And Mrs. Cooper, could you say just a word about the homework? I mean, why is it important, if you think it is, for Jay-lynn to be getting it done?

MRS. COOPER: I just want to make sure she doesn't fall behind the rest of the class by not having a chance to practice the material we learn during the day.

ASSISTANT PRINCIPAL: I see. So it's an issue of having time to practice. I wonder if there's anything we can do so that Jaylynn gets time to practice what she's learning in school, but without putting any more on Ms. Jordan or the neighbor's plates, which are already very full. Any ideas?

GUIDANCE COUNSELOR: Well, we do have after-school homework club. Parents signed up for it at the beginning of the year, but we didn't get a sign-up sheet back, so we assumed Jaylynn wasn't participating. I wonder now whether that would work. The only problem is that Jaylynn would need a ride home at 4:30—there's no after-school bus.

MS. JORDAN: Well, I could probably get my neighbor to pick her up if it meant not having Jaylynn for an hour and a half after school!

ASSISTANT PRINCIPAL: And Mrs. Cooper, if Jaylynn was getting in her practice at homework club, would that work for you?

MRS. COOPER: Yes, I can't see any problem with that, as long as she is getting the practice somewhere.

ASSISTANT PRINCIPAL: Well, that sounds like a great, flexible solution that works for everyone. Ms. Jordan, I know you need to get going, but would you like us to present this to Jaylynn or would you prefer to do that? Hopefully she will think it's a good idea too, but we need to make sure she doesn't have any concerns about the plan before we run with it.

MS. JORDAN: You can talk to her about it and let me know when I should talk to my neighbor.

In this scenario, the assistant principal, who was certified in CPS, reminded her staff of the underlying philosophy that *people are doing the best they can with the skills they have*, and that when parents don't meet our expectations, rather than fall back on Plan A, it is best to remain empathic and try to understand their perspective about the problem. She facilitated a Plan B conversation that not only addressed the problem at hand (homework) but also went a long way toward building a collaborative alliance between home and school. Clearly, there are more problems to solve here in the future, but now the team and Ms. Jordan have some success under their belt, and a better relationship too, thanks to Collaborative Problem Solving.

# CHAPTER 15
## DATA MATTER: WHAT THE RESEARCH SHOWS

*Mrs. Berry, director of special education for the district, is known for being fair, but tough. She is also someone who believes strongly in using evidence-based approaches. "Show me the data!" she demands of her colleagues who come back from their CPS introductory training excited to advocate for training everyone in the model. "I can't dedicate time and resources to everyone learning an approach unless I can be confident it will work!"*

In this chapter, we review the evidence base for CPS and some of the implications for your use of the approach. Since CPS is now widely used in many schools and therapeutic systems across the world, few people remember that it began as a parenting approach. The first empirical study of CPS as a parenting approach was a randomized controlled clinical trial conducted in the Psychiatry Department at Massachusetts General Hospital (Greene, Ablon, & Goring, 2003; Greene, Ablon, Goring, et al., 2004). In this study, families with children who had a diagnosis of oppositional defiant disorder (ODD) and significant mood symptoms received individual family treatment either with CPS or Parent Management Training (PMT), a behavioral approach that focuses on reducing oppositional behavior by motivating children to be more compliant. Results indicated that CPS was associated with significant improvements in parents' perceptions of competence and stress and in parent-child interactions, as well as a reduction in oppositional behaviors. Children in the CPS condition were rated as improving significantly more than children in the PMT condition, by both therapist (measured post-intervention) and parent (measured at follow-up). In many other variables, improvements experienced by families receiving CPS were at least as good as those experienced by families receiving PMT. The authors concluded that the CPS model was a worthy alternative to behavioral models such as PMT (Greene, Ablon, & Goring, 2003; Greene, Ablon, Goring, et al., 2004). Knowing how successful CPS can be for parents is helpful for educators, who often hear firsthand about struggles at home as well. Pointing parents toward resources for them to learn the model can be greatly appreciated and do a world of good for your students when they leave school. Obviously, the more CPS happens outside school, the more chance there is to build those skills.

So how did this successful parenting approach gain widespread use outside of parenting circles? The first systematic implementation of CPS was in a locked inpatient psychiatry unit in Massachusetts for children ages three to 14 who were at acute risk of harming themselves or someone else. A large percentage of the children admitted exhibited severe oppositional behavior, and many had experienced significant trauma. Prior to the implementation of CPS, the unit experienced a rate of mechanical restraints, locked-door seclusions, as well as staff and patient injuries that was well above the state average. In this first sitewide implementation attempt, thirty-four staff members were trained in CPS and attended supervision sessions twice a week for one year. Following CPS implementation, documented restraints, short physical holds, and injuries decreased significantly (Greene, Ablon, & Martin, 2006; Regan, Curtin, & Vorderer, 2006). The results of this study led to many other similar inpatient units seeking to implement the approach. Soon, others reported consistent results (Martin, Krieg, Esposito, Stubbe, & Cardona, 2008; Mohr, Olson, Martin, & Pumariega, 2009).

Since youth from inpatient programs are often discharged to residential programs and therapeutic day schools, these types of programs soon began to take note of the dramatic results that could be obtained through use of CPS. As a result, in the years that followed, use of the approach began to spread throughout numerous therapeutic systems. Results in these programs suggested that, as in inpatient facilities, using

CPS was associated with a reduction in restrictive interventions like physical restraints and seclusion, as well as reduced staff and child injuries. In addition, one study found that CPS was associated with improved social skills and community engagement, and reductions in internalizing as well as externalizing symptoms (Pollastri et al., 2013; Pollastri, Lieberman, Boldt, & Ablon, 2016). These results are helpful to keep in mind when working with your most challenging students, for whom it is often easy to lose hope and wonder if anything could help. CPS has proven effective with the most challenging and traumatized youth.

After residential programs and therapeutic day schools, the use of CPS spread to less-restrictive settings, including alternative schools and special education programs housed within mainstream educational settings. These programs sought a solution for the students who exhibited chronic challenging behaviors and who were the most frequent recipients of school discipline. Like in the inpatient and residential programs, many evaluations of outcomes in schools during this time focused on documenting the reduction of punitive consequences for students' challenging behavior, such as restraints and seclusion, office referrals, detentions, and suspensions, and there were consistent reductions in these strategies after adopting CPS. For instance, one regional school program for elementary students with emotional disorders in Maryland reported that after the adoption of CPS, there was a dramatic decrease in restraints as well as minutes spent in time out. After schoolwide implementation of CPS in a community-based educational program for middle and high school students with emotional and behavioral disorders in Oregon, the rate of restraint/seclusion decreased significantly, and after three years, continuation of the CPS program in these schools resulted in a virtual elimination of these disciplinary practices. Finally, at a program implemented in an Oregon public school system for students displaying oppositional behaviors, adoption of CPS was associated with significantly fewer minutes spent in out-of-class coaching, supervised isolation, and the de-escalation room (Pollastri et al., 2013).

While most studies of CPS in schools focused simply on measuring reductions in punitive discipline, a few teams have explored other hypothesized changes. At an alternative school in New York that serves students with severe behavior and/or academic challenges, in addition to observing a dramatic reduction in the number of suspensions per year, administrators reported a substantial increase in school attendance and a significant increase in family participation after CPS was introduced (Pollastri et al., 2013). Additionally, staff in an alternative middle school program in Colorado examined whether training teachers in CPS would result in a reduction of teacher stress related to particularly challenging 7th and 8th grade students. In this pilot study, eight teachers received 12 hours of training, then participated in 75-minute weekly consultations for eight weeks. Each teacher was asked to target two students on whom to focus their practice of the intervention. After four months, in addition to observing a reduction in discipline referrals, teacher stress decreased significantly, and this result was strongest for teachers who were rated most competent in the practice of CPS (Schaubman, Stetson, & Plog, 2011). Five years later, the same team published the results of a follow-up study that extended the sample and outcomes examined. Here, they tracked 34 staff in six behavior development programs serving students whose social-emotional and behavioral needs required more intensive support than a general education setting could provide. Again, teachers who learned CPS reported significantly reduced stress when working with challenging students. Further, both parent and student reports indicated a reduction in problem behaviors, and results suggested that students built skills in the areas of behavior regulation and emotional control (Stetson & Plog, 2016). These are some of the myriad outcomes that you can reasonably expect to see with successful implementation of CPS. Hopefully reviewing these results will help you to identify which outcomes are of most interest to you during your implementation process so you can track them as you go.

Most recently, in response to the growing body of research on the effectiveness of the CPS approach in schools as well as other settings, initiatives have begun to extend the reach of CPS to other novel settings. For example, the New York Police Department will provide intensive CPS training to more than 3,000 school safety officers and agents in New York City in the next few years, with the intention of decreasing the use of punitive discipline in the city's schools, up to and including in-school arrest. After a 2013 pilot project in which CPS exposure training was provided to more than 5,000 officers and agents, crime, summonses, and in-school arrests were reported to decrease dramatically. Further research will need to evaluate the extent to which CPS in particular is contributing to an improved school climate in New York City.

Although we are always in need of larger, rigorous studies on the outcomes associated with CPS implementation in schools, the evidence is consistent and promising. Thus, as the empirical evidence of the impact of CPS continues to grow, we have also begun to examine more nuanced questions, such as the relationship between use of CPS and academic gains, whether CPS can be used to reduce the racial and ethnic disproportionality of punitive school discipline, and which components of the approach are most predictive of positive outcomes. We also hope to investigate whether implementation of CPS in schools is associated with cost savings as has been suggested by research on CPS in other settings (Pollastri, Lieberman, Boldt & Ablon, 2016) and as has been found for other school-based interventions (Belfield et al., 2015). We expect results in these areas to continue to impact the ways we teach and implement CPS in schools.

# AFTERWORD

Great progress has been made in the past several decades when it comes to better understanding and more effectively intervening with students who have learning differences. Gone are the days when teachers instruct in a one-size-fits-all way. It is commonly accepted that to teach effectively, one must individualize instructional strategies to meet the needs of different students. However, differentiating instruction is hard! Especially when you have 28 students in your class and statewide mandates to meet with so little time. And yet, the goal of differentiated instruction is a critical and worthwhile one toward which we strive.

In this book, we have argued that working with students with behavioral challenges should be no different, and brain science backs us up. We no longer are deterred from individualizing instruction because of perceived unfairness; it is only when it comes to behavior that we tend to get stuck. However, when you realize that challenging behavior is just another form of a learning disability (i.e., a skills deficit), it makes it easier to understand and explain doing something different for a student who needs assistance with certain skills. Thankfully, these days, we would never stop sending a student to the reading specialist if other students objected that it's unfair that she gets to leave class. We simply need to extend this thinking to the realm of challenging behavior. The future is differentiated discipline. It is high time that students with behavioral challenges receive the same humane, accurate, and effective interventions as students with recognized learning disabilities who historically lost out with one-size-fits-all teaching.

Perhaps the students for whom traditional school discipline has the

*The future is differentiated discipline.*

most disastrous effects and who most deserve differentiated discipline are the very students who already have the deck stacked against them: students of color and students from disadvantaged economic environments. If students with behavioral challenges are harmed by traditional school discipline, these students take the brunt of that damage. Across the United States, students of color are suspended at disproportionately high rates for much less serious offenses than their Caucasian peers (American Psychological Association Zero Tolerance Task Force, 2008). Data released in March 2012 by the Office of Civil Rights indicate that more than 70 percent of the students involved in school-related arrests or referred to law enforcement were Hispanic or black (Transformed Civil Rights Data Collection, 2012). Black students are between 1.25 and 9 times more likely to be suspended, 1.04 to 8.97 times more likely to be expelled, and 1.58 to 11.53 times more likely to enter the juvenile justice system than white juveniles (varying by state; Skiba et al., 2003). In New York City alone, black students represent 33 percent of the student population, but have accounted for 53 percent of suspensions in the last decade (Miller et al., 2011). How does this happen? One theory stems from research indicating that teachers' implicit biases can lead to making judgments about students' behaviors. Specifically, teachers often implicitly attribute the actions of students of color as intentional or malicious, particularly in subjective situations that allow room for more judgment (Gilbert & Gay, 1985; Weinstein, Tomlinson-Clarke, & Curran, 2004). In other words, implicit racist biases inherent in our society lead teachers to think *will not skill!* As a result, teachers are significantly more likely to foresee themselves suspending a student of color (Okonofua & Eberhardt, 2015). There is also evidence that teachers perceive students who appear to be from lower-income families to be of lower academic standing (McCombs and Gay, 1988), to be less likely to have successful futures (Auwarter and Aruguete, 2008) and to be worthy of lower expectations (Harvey & Slatin, 1975; Rosenthal & Jacobson, 1992), independent of perceived racial/ethnic background. These students are then also at risk of having their behaviors misjudged as more intentional, leading to more punitive discipline. CPS offers a potential solution to this problem. Helping teachers understand challenging behaviors accurately, through the lens of a lag in skill development, not a lack of will, holds great promise to reduce the massive human and societal costs of disproportionate discipline.

Like differentiated instruction, differentiating discipline will be hard. It will require work to avoid falling back on a one-size-fits-all code of conduct and a menu of preordained punishments when those expectations aren't met. Inevitably, the obstacles we have described in this book will rise up to challenge educators who try to make this change. We used to say that transforming school discipline was like trying to turn an aircraft carrier around in a canal. In one of the first schools to adopt CPS, the music teacher became among the biggest CPS champions. She went on to teach science, to become an assistant principal and then a principal, and ultimately to complete her certification in CPS. Along the way, she brought us a picture of an aircraft carrier turning around in a canal. Reflecting upon her experience trying to help her colleagues rethink school discipline, she noted that you can indeed be successful if you take it slow but steady, enlist everybody on board, and get help from people around the ship as well.

We are now in the uncomfortable space when knowledge has emerged, but practice has not yet changed. We know that traditional school discipline is ineffective for the students who encounter it the most, and we know why. Translating that knowledge into practice requires bravery, persistence, and the willingness to not only confront, but to cause, distress in a system. Remember what we said earlier: No pain, no gain. Students with behavioral challenges have endured too much pain at the hands of traditional school discipline. As educators, we owe it to them to endure a pain that pales in comparison: the pain required to rethink and to fix school discipline.

# APPENDIX A

## Collaborative Problem Solving®
### Assessment and Planning Tool (CPS-APT)

Student's Name _____     Date _____

### ASSESSMENT: Identifying Challenging Behaviors, Problems, and Skill Struggles

Responding to life's demands requires a lot of thinking skills. If a student doesn't have the skills to handle a problem, it is likely to result in some form of challenging behavior.

**Use this tool to make 3 lists:**

List #1: Challenging behaviors.

List #2: Specific problems that lead to challenging behaviors.

List #3: Skills to be developed (see following page)

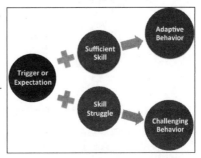

| PLAN A, B, or C | PROBLEMS ✛ | SKILL STRUGGLES ➡ | CHALLENGING BEHAVIORS |
|---|---|---|---|
| | The situations **WHEN** the student has difficulty. Also known as expectations, precipitants, antecedents, triggers or contexts that can lead to challenging behavior. When making your list, describe the who, what, when and where, and be *specific!* | The reasons the student is having difficulty handling these specific situations. Use the list of problems as your clues, and refer to the list of skills on the next page. If the problems are the *WHEN*, the lagging skills are the **WHY**. | The challenging responses that often bring up the greatest concerns for adults and parents. Examples are yelling, swearing, refusing, hitting, crying, shutting down etc. |
| | **List #2** | **List #3** | **List #1** |
| | | | |

# CPS SKILLS REFERENCE SHEET

## Language and Communication Skills

- Understands spoken directions
- Understands and follows conversations
- Expresses concerns, needs, or thoughts in words
- Is able to tell someone what's bothering him or her

## Attention and Working Memory Skills

- Stays with tasks requiring sustained attention
- Does things in a logical sequence or set order
- Keeps track of time; correctly assesses how much time a task will take
- Reflects on multiple thoughts or ideas at the same time
- Maintains focus during activities
- Ignores irrelevant noises, people, or other stimuli; tunes things out when necessary
- Considers a range of solutions to a problem

## Emotion- and Self-Regulation Skills

- Thinks rationally, even when frustrated
- Manages irritability in an age-appropriate way
- Manages anxiety in an age-appropriate way
- Manages disappointment in an age-appropriate way
- Thinks before responding; considers the likely outcomes or consequences of his/her actions
- Can adjust his/her arousal level to meet the demands of a situation (e.g., calming after recess or after getting upset, falling asleep/waking up, staying seated during class or meals, etc.)

## Cognitive Flexibility Skills

- Handles transitions, shifts easily from one task to another
- Is able to see "shades of gray" rather than thinking only in "black-and-white"
- Thinks hypothetically, is able to envision different possibilities
- Handles deviations from rules, routines, and original plans
- Handles unpredictability, ambiguity, uncertainty, and novelty
- Can shift away from an original idea, solution, or plan
- Takes into account situational factors that may mean a change in plans (Example: "If it rains, we may need to cancel.")
- Interprets information accurately/<u>avoids</u> over-generalizing or personalizing (Example: <u>Avoids</u> saying "Everyone's out to get me," "Nobody likes me," "You always blame me," "It's not fair," "I'm stupid," or "Things will never work out for me.")

## Social Thinking Skills

- Pays attention to verbal and nonverbal social cues
- Accurately interprets nonverbal social cues (like facial expressions and tone of voice)
- Starts conversations with peers, enters groups of peers appropriately
- Seeks attention in appropriate ways
- Understands how his or her behavior affects other people
- Understands how he or she is coming across or being perceived by others
- Empathizes with others, appreciates others' perspectives or points of view

## PLANNING: Prioritizing Problems

Next, decide which Problems are the first to be addressed with Plan B. Mark those Problems with ⒷB in the leftmost column. Not sure where to start? Use these guidelines:

Do you have a good relationship with the student?

YES → Start with the Problems causing the most frequent or severe challenging behavior

NO → Start with Problems that will be easiest to address, that you feel most flexible about, or that the child is most invested in

For Problems that you won't address using Plan B right away, mark with Ⓐ or Ⓒ (for now).

- Choose Plan A if trying to get your expectation met is more important than reducing challenging behavior.
- Choose Plan C if reducing challenging behavior is more important than getting the expectation met for now.

REMINDER: As problems get solved using Plan B, you will choose new problems from those marked A and C to be addressed next with Plan B.

These tools are regularly evaluated and improved. Please check the website or contact Think:Kids for latest versions.

# APPENDIX B

## Plan B Prep Sheet

### GENERAL PLANNING

**WHAT** is the focus of the conversation (*the problem to be solved not the challenging behavior!*)?

_____

**WHO** is going to have the conversation?

_____

**WHEN**, **WHERE** and **WHILE DOING WHAT** are you going to have the conversation?

_____

### INGREDIENT #1: EMPATHIZE

HOW ARE YOU GOING TO START THE CONVERSATION AND FRAME THE PROBLEM? Be specific about the problem but don't focus on the behavior, assume or blame.

- o Stick to the facts or externalize the problem.
- o Examples: "I've noticed that..."
  "...waking up has been tough lately,"
  "...something's been up with work,"
  "...something about group hasn't been working for you lately,"
  "...something about the food seems to be bothering you,"
  "...something about family visits has been tough,"
- o Finish by asking, "Can you fill me in?" or "What's going on?

Write down opening statement here:

_____

(NOTE: Complete next section **ONLY** if you anticipate the individual having difficulty expressing his/her concerns)

DO YOU HAVE ANY IDEA WHAT THE PERSON'S CONCERNS MIGHT BE?

- o What types of clarifying questions might you ask / educated guesses might you make if needed?

### INGREDIENT #2: SHARE YOUR CONCERN

WHY ARE YOU BRINGING THE PROBLEM UP?

- o Clarify your concerns ahead of time. Be specific and concise! **Health, safety, learning, impact on others**? Write down how exactly you will communicate them to the individual here:

_____

These tools are regularly evaluated and improved. Please check
www.thinkkids.org or contact Think:Kids for latest versions.

# APPENDIX C

Think:Kids

**CPS INTEGRITY**

SCORECARD

Date:_____ Trainee's Name:_____ Evaluator's Name: _____

Organization:_____ Group/Team:_____

| | TO CONSIDER... | Skillfulness Rating (4= High, 1= Low) | Notes |
|---|---|---|---|
| 1 | **ASSESSMENT**<br>• Classified problems , skills struggles, and challenging behaviors correctly<br>• Identified specific triggers or unmet expectations as problems<br>• Hypothesized about skill struggles that contribute to challenging behavior | ☐ 4<br>☐ 3<br>☐ 2<br>☐ 1<br>☐ N/A | |
| 2 | **PLANNING**<br>• Assigned Plan B for at least 1 problem to be solved, with a rationale for doing so<br>• Assigned a Plan to be used for all other problems to be solved and discussed how you will do Plans A or C<br>• Discussed need to clarify expectations, modify environment, or gather more information when necessary | ☐ 4<br>☐ 3<br>☐ 2<br>☐ 1<br>☐ N/A | |
| 3 | **INTERVENTION** - Step #1: *Empathize*<br>• Started Plan B with a neutral statement about the *problem* (not behavior!)<br>• Used 4 tools (1. Clarifying questions, 2. Educated guessing, 3. Reflective listening, 4. Reassurance) to clarify youth's concern(s) | ☐ 4<br>☐ 3<br>☐ 2<br>☐ 1<br>☐ N/A | |
| | **INTERVENTION** - Step #2: *Share*<br>• Shared adult's specific *concern* (not solution!) | ☐ 4<br>☐ 3<br>☐ 2<br>☐ 1<br>☐ N/A | |
| | **INTERVENTION** - Step #3: *Collaborate*<br>• Invited youth to brainstorm solutions that address both concerns and gave youth first opportunity<br>• Evaluated solutions together with youth<br>• Responded to dysregulation with reflective listening and reassurance when needed | ☐ 4<br>☐ 3<br>☐ 2<br>☐ 1<br>☐ N/A | |
| 4 | **PHILOSOPHY**<br>• Portrayed belief that challenging behaviors arise from skill not will<br>• Avoided use of behavioral/operant strategies | ☐ 4<br>☐ 3<br>☐ 2<br>☐ 1<br>☐ N/A | |
| | **GLOBAL CPS INTEGRITY SCORE:** | ☐ 4<br>☐ 3<br>☐ 2<br>☐ 1 | |

These tools are regularly evaluated and improved. Please check
www.thinkkids.org or contact Think:Kids for latest versions.

# REFERENCES

Abel, M. H., & Sewell, J. (1999). Stress and burnout in rural and urban secondary school teachers. *The journal of educational research*, *92*(5), 287-293.

Ablon, J. S. (2018). *Changeable: How Collaborative Problem Solving Changes Lives at Home, at School, and at Work*. New York: Penguin Random House.

Alexander, M. (2011). Applying Implementation Research to Improve Community Corrections: Making Sure That New Thing Sticks. *Fed. Probation*, *75*, 47.

Alexander, K. L., Entwisle, D. R., & Horsey, C. S. (1997). From first grade forward: Early foundations of high school dropout. *Sociology of education*, 87-107.

American Psychological Association Zero Tolerance Task Force. (2008). Are zero tolerance policies effective in the schools?: an evidentiary review and recommendations. *The American Psychologist, 63*(9), 852.

Auwarter, A. E., & Aruguete, M. S. (2008). Effects of student gender and socioeconomic status on teacher perceptions. *The Journal of Educational Research, 101*(4), 242–246.

Balas, E. A., & Boren, S. A. (2000). *Managing clinical knowledge for health care improvement*. Yearbook of medical informatics 2000: patient-centered systems.

Beck, A. T. (1976). *Cognitive therapies and emotional disorders.* New York: New American Library.

Becker, K. D, Chorpita, B. F., Daleiden, E. L. (2011). Improvement in symptoms versus functioning: How do our best treatments measure up? *Administration and Policy in Mental Health, 38*(6), 440–458.

Belfield, C., Bowden, A. B., Klapp, A., Levin, H., Shand, R., & Zander, S. (2015). The economic value of social and emotional learning. *Journal of Benefit-Cost Analysis*, 6(3), 508-544.

Boyle, G. J., Borg, M. G., Falzon, J. M., & Baglioni, A. J. (1995). A structural model of the dimensions of teacher stress. *British Journal of Educational Psychology, 65*(1), 49-67.

Burns, D. D. (2012). *Feeling good: The new mood therapy.* New York: New American Library.

Deci, E. L., Koestner, R., & Ryan, R. M. (2001). Extrinsic rewards and intrinsic motivation in education: Reconsidered once again. *Review of educational research, 71*(1), 1-27.

Duckworth, A. (2016). *Grit: The power of passion and perseverance.* Simon and Schuster.

Felitti, V. J., Anda, R. F., Nordenberg, D., Williamson, D. F., Spitz, A. M., Edwards, V., . . . & Marks, J. S. (1998). Relationship of childhood abuse and household dysfunction to many of the leading causes of death in adults: The Adverse Childhood Experiences (ACE) Study. *American journal of preventive medicine, 14*(4), 245-258.

Fixsen, D. L., Blase, K. A., Timbers, G. D., & Wolf, M. M. (2001). In search of program implementation: 792 replications of the Teaching-Family Model. *Offender rehabilitation in practice: Implementing and evaluating effective programs*, 149-166.

Gilbert, S. E., & Gay, G. (1985). Improving the success in school of poor black children. *Phi Delta Kappan, 67*(2), 133–137.

Greene, R. W. (1998). *The explosive child : a new approach for understanding and parenting easily frustrated, "chronically inflexible" children* (1st ed.). New York: HarperCollins Publishers.

Greene, R. W. (2005). *The explosive child : a new approach for understanding and parenting easily frustrated, "chronically inflexible" children* (3rd ed.). New York: HarperCollins Publishers.

Greene, R. W., & Ablon, J. S. (2005). *Treating explosive kids: The Collaborative Problem-Solving approach*. Guilford Press.

Greene, R. W., Ablon, J. S., & Goring, J. C. (2003). A transactional model of oppositional behavior: Underpinnings of the Collaborative Problem Solving approach. *Journal of psychosomatic research, 55*(1), 67-75.

Greene, R. W., Ablon, J. S., & Martin, A. (2006). Use of collaborative problem solving to reduce seclusion and restraint in child and adolescent inpatient units. *Psychiatric Services, 57*(5), 610-612.

Greene, R. W., Ablon J. S., Monuteaux, M. C., Goring, J. C., Henin, A., Raezer-Blakely, L., Edwards, G., Markey, J., & Biederman, J. (2004). Effectiveness of collaborative problem solving in affectively dysregulated children with oppositional defiant disorder: Initial findings. *Journal of Consulting and Clinical Psychology, 72*(6), 1157–1164.

Harvey, D. G., & Slatin, G. T. (1975). The relationship between child's SES and teacher expectations: A test of the middle-class bias hypothesis. *Social Forces, 54*(1), 140–159.

Heifetz, R. A. (1994). *Leadership without easy answers* (Vol. 465). Harvard University Press.

Joyce, B. R., & Showers, B. (2002). Student achievement through staff development. In B. Joyce & B. Showers (Eds), *Student achievement through staff development* (69–94). Alexandria, VA: ASCD.

Kleim, J. A., & Jones, T. A. (2008). Principles of experience-dependent neural plasticity: implications for rehabilitation after brain damage. *Journal of speech, language, and hearing research*, 51(1), S225-S239.

Martin, A., Krieg, H., Esposito, F., Stubbe, D., & Cardona, L. (2008). Reduction of restraint and seclusion through collaborative problem solving: a five-year prospective inpatient study. *Psychiatric Services*, *59*(12), 1406-1412.

Martin, D. J., Garske, J. P., & Davis, M. K. (2000). Relation of the therapeutic alliance with outcome and other variables: A meta-analytic review. *Journal of Consulting and Clinical Psychology*, 68(3), 438-450.

McCombs, R. C., & Gay, J. (1988). Effects of race, class, and IQ information on judgments of parochial grade school teachers. *The Journal of Social Psychology, 128*(5), 647–652.

Miller, J., Ofer, U., Artz, A., Bahl, T., Foster, T., Phenix, D., & Thomas, H. A. (2011). *Education interrupted: The growing use of suspensions in New York City's public schools.* New York: New York Civil Liberties Union.

Mohr, W. K., Martin, A., Olson, J. N., Pumariega, A. J., & Branca, N. (2009). Beyond point and level systems: Moving toward child-centered programming. *American Journal of Orthopsychiatry, 79*(1), 8.

Okonofua, J. A., & Eberhardt, J. L. (2015). Two strikes race and the disciplining of young students. *Psychological Science, 26*(5), 617–624.

Perry, B. D. (2006). *The Neurosequential Model of Therapeutics Phase I Certification Manual (version 1.1).* Houston, TX: CTA Press.

Perry, B. D. & Ablon, J. S. (2014) *Through the Prism: Synthesizing evidence-Based Neuro-Cognitive Models.* Presentation, Salem, OR.

Pollastri, A. R., Epstein, L. D., Heath, G. H., & Ablon, J. S. (2013). The Collaborative Problem Solving approach: Outcomes across settings. *Harvard Review of Psychiatry, 21*(4), 188–199.

Pollastri, A. R., Lieberman, R. E., Boldt, S. L., & Ablon, J. S. (2016). Minimizing Seclusion and Restraint in Youth Residential and Day Treatment Through Site-Wide Implementation of Collaborative Problem Solving. *Residential Treatment for Children & Youth, 33*(3-4), 186-205.

Pollastri, A. R., Lieberman, R. E., Boldt, S. L., & Ablon, J. S. (2016). Minimizing seclusion and restraint in youth residential and day treatment through site-wide implementation of Collaborative Problem Solving. *Residential Treatment for Children & Youth,* 33(3-4), 186-205.

Pollastri, A. R., Wang, L., Vuijk, P. J., Hill, E. N., Lee, B. A., Samkavitz, A., Braaten, E. B., Ablon, J. S., & Doyle, A. E. (2018). *Reliability and validity of the Thinking Skills Inventory, a screening tool for skill deficits in youth with behavioral challenges.* Manuscript submitted for publication.

Regan, K. M., Curtin, C., & Vorderer, L. (2006). Paradigm Shifts in Inpatient Psychiatric Care of Children: Approaching Child-and Family-Centered Care. *Journal of Child and Adolescent Psychiatric Nursing, 19*(1), 29-40.

Rosenthal, R., & Jacobson, L. (1992). *Pygmalion in the classroom: Teacher expectation and pupils' intellectual development.* Norwalk, CT: Crown House Publishing.

Ross, M. E. (2010). Designing and using program evaluation as a tool for reform. *Journal of Research on Leadership Education, 5*(12.7), 481–506.

Ryan, R. M., & Deci, E. L. (2000). Self-determination theory and the facilitation of intrinsic motivation, social development, and well-being. *American psychologist, 55*(1), 68.

Scaccia, J. P., Cook, B. S., Lamont, A., Wandersman, A., Castellow, J., Katz, J., & Beidas, R. S. (2015). A practical implementation science heuristic for organizational readiness: R= MC2. *Journal of Community Psychology, 43*(4), 484-501.

Schaubman, A., Stetson, E., Plog, A. (2016). Reducing teacher stress by implementing Collaborative Problem Solving in schools: Results of a year-long consultation project. *School Social Work Journal*, 35(2), 72–93.

Schaubman, A., Stetson, E., Plog, A. (2011). Reducing teacher stress by implementing Collaborative Problem Solving in a school setting. *School Social Work Journal, 35*(2), 72–93.

Shonkoff, J. P., Garner, A. S., Siegel, B. S., Dobbins, M. I., Earls, M. F., McGuinn, L., ... & Committee on Early Childhood, Adoption, and Dependent Care. (2012). The lifelong effects of early childhood adversity and toxic stress. *Pediatrics, 129*(1), e232-e246.

Skiba, R. J., Simmons, A., Staudinger, L., Rausch, M., Dow, G., & Feggins, R. (2003). *Consistent removal: Contributions of school discipline to the school-prison pipeline.* School to Prison Pipeline Conference, Boston, MA.

Stetson, E. A., & Plog, A. E. (2016). Collaborative Problem Solving in Schools: Results of a Year-Long Consultation Project. *School Social Work Journal, 40*(2).

Soper, D. W., & Combs, A. W. (1962). The helping relationship as seen by teachers and therapists. *Journal of consulting psychology, 26*(3), 288.

Transformed Civil Rights Data Collection. (2012, March 12). Retrieved July 20, 2016, from http://ocrdata.ed.gov/Downloads/CMOCRTheTrans formedCRDCFINAL3-15-12Accessible-1.pdf.

Vygotsky, L. S. (1978). *Mind in society: The development of higher psychological processes* (M. Cole, V. John-Steiner, S. Scribner & E. Souberman., Eds.) (A. R. Luria, M. Lopez-Morillas & M. Cole [with J. V. Wertsch], Trans.) Cambridge, Mass.: Harvard University Press. (Original manuscripts [ca. 1930-1934])

Weinstein, C. S., Tomlinson-Clarke, S., & Curran, M. (2004). Toward a conception of culturally responsive classroom management. *Journal of Teacher Education, 55*(1), 25–38.

# INDEX

Note: *Italicized* page locators refer to illustrations; boxes are noted in parentheses.

good, 81, 84, 140

moderate and predictable, brain change and, 81

neural networks of brain and, 79–80

teacher, CPS and reduction in, 166

titrating, via dosing and spacing, 85–86

toxic, 79

unpleasant interactions with parents and, 158

stress response

activating safely, 81

motivational strategies and, 13

system, 78

students of color, traditional school discipline and, 14, 170

supervisors, skills assessment of supervisees and, 154

surprises, small Group Plan B and, 121

suspensions

CPS and reduced rates of, 166

disciplinary practice changes and, 5

students of color and rates of, 170

teachers, students of color and biases of, 170

teacher stress

behavioral challenges in the classroom and, 3

reduced, change in disciplinary practices and, 5

team meeting, consensus building, BIP process, and, 51

team recruitment, for schoolwide change and implementation, 134

temporal lobe, of brain, 76

texting in class, small Group Plan B example, 120–23

therapeutic day schools, research studies on CPS in, 164–65

thinking skill, traditional functional behavior analysis *vs.* CPS Assessment, 16 (box)

Thinking Skills Inventory (TSI), 138

thinking traps (cognitive distortions), types of, 28

Think:Kids

latest versions of CPS-APT, *173*

latest versions of CPS Integrity Scorecard, *177*

latest versions of CPS Skills Reference Sheet, *174*

latest versions Plan B Prep Sheet, *175*

three Rs of information processing, mapping Plan B steps onto, 82–83, 83 (box)

time for Plan B, finding, 143–45

time outs, CPS and reduction in, 165

token economy or reward systems, 12

tough problems, troubleshooting Plan B and, 97

toxic stress, 79

traditional school discipline

broken nature of, 4

CPS-related teamwork *vs.*, 147

limits of, 11–13